MW01248750

Reaching for the

Light

Reaching for the Light
Copyright © 2016 Anne Lesley Lanier

All rights reserved. No part of this book may be reproduced
(except for inclusion in reviews), disseminated or utilized in
any form or by any means, electronic or mechanical, including
photocopying, recording, or in any information storage and
retrieval system, or the Internet/World Wide Web without
written permission from the author or publisher.

Cover Photos by Rob Dutton
flagstaffrob@yahoo.com

Printed in the United States of America
First Edition Printing

Design by
Arbor Services, Inc.
http://www.arborservices.co/

Reaching for the Light
Anne Lesley Lanier

ISBN: 978-0-692-59857-3
LCCN: 2015920677
1. Title 2. Author 3. Poetry

INTRODUCTION

These writings are reflections on the journey taken over the two years after my son Chris took his life. This journey has been and continues to be a messy, confusing, and unpredictable path to walk. It has been a crazy-making experience at times, one that has taken me to the darkest of places. As I keep reaching for the light, this new life has taken me back and forth, up and down, around and around and around all the emotions of grief: the shock, the denial, the anger, the bargaining, the acceptance. Sometimes I have been through all those emotions in five minutes or in one day, and I never know when the waves will come. It seems to be never ending, but the circles around do get a little bit wider with time. And I am learning that you can "be broken and blessed, hurting and healing, lost and found, doubting and yearning to believe"* and that there is light, no matter the darkness, there is light.

*The Very Rev. Dr. Lisa Tucker-Gray

DEDICATION

For you reading this . . . may you "slip beneath the still surface on the well of grief" and may you "find the small gold coins thrown by" this mom "who wished for something else." May you find love and gratitude, may you find forgiveness in the hurt, clarity in the confusion, hope in the despair, faith in the doubt, joy in the sadness, light in the darkness. I wish you peace and joy in quiet moments.

OTHER BOOKS BY ANNE

Table of Contents

A Quivering Inside

The pain within some endings
Is searing, burning
It takes your breath away
Makes you fall to your knees
The words you did not say
Haunting you
The things you didn't do
Crushing you
The memories of your last visit
Replaying endlessly in your mind
And yet
There is a quivering inside
Something that tells you all will be well
That there will be a new beginning
"Like the legend of the phoenix
All ends with beginnings
What keeps the planet spinning
The force of love beginning"*

*lyrics from *Get Lucky* by Pharrell Williams and Nile Rodgers

Silence

Sometimes the only place to stand is in the heartbreak
Looking out
With questions of the heart
Seeking answers where there are none
And so there is silence
The deep silence of pain
And if we surrender to it
There will be stillness
There will be calm
There will be peace

Waiting for Time to Move On

I think I want time to move
Get me away from this pain
But no, wait, the faster time moves
The further away I get from my son, my Chris, my heart
Please stop time unfolding
I want to go back
Back to before this nightmare began
Back to when I held you in my arms
But no, time keeps moving
Time keeps running out
Away from this moment, away from this pain
And maybe
Time moves toward healing
Toward being close again
To resting
To comfort
Closer to beginning again

Frozen

I was frozen in time
The words made no sense
My daughter on the other end of the phone
"He shot himself, Mom! He shot himself"
And that is when I became frozen in time
Repeated the Thich Nhat Hanh words
"I have arrived, I am home"
I accessed the strongest, most courageous part of myself
"I have arrived, I am home"
I came home to darkness
I came home to love and connection, yes
But I came home to one heart frozen
One heart breaking
Home to heartbreak, upon heartbreak, upon heartbreak

Home to Heartbreak

We must learn to comfort ourselves
Learn how to be strong and courageous
How to rest
Especially in the heartbreak
When the journey is inward
When you must attend to your altar
When you have arrived
When you are home
Home to heartbreak and loss
This is the wintertime
I am asked to witness what no mother perhaps should
      witness
But I had to show my child
I would witness everything
No matter what, he had to know
I would not leave him
Would never have left him
I would have stayed
He had only to have stayed with us
But he could not stay
Said it was his time to go
And so
My Chris, my heart
I witness everything to honor you, to honor your death and
      dying
I hold you always with love and compassion and in sacred
      space
I went with you to the places perhaps you thought you would
      go alone

I have arrived, I am home
I identified your body, my love
I viewed the pictures as you lay in the field—lifeless
I bow to you, I honor you
I am here
There was blood, yes, but what I saw was you sleeping, lying
   on your stomach, your head cradled in your arms
Still holding your phone in your hand, the phone with your
   last cry for help
In the other hand, the gun
Oh dear God a gun
How could this be?
A hole behind your ear, dry blood, jelled blood
Eyes closed
Eyes closed . . . thank God . . . eyes closed
My child sleeping, sleeping
No more struggle, no more suffering, no more fighting your
   demons, no more fear
My mind cries NO! NO! NO!
I try to put everything in order
If I can create order—everything will be all right,
   we will be safe
I beg of time to stop unfolding
Please stop unfolding
I make plans for a beautiful Memorial Service
Open casket
Everyone can say good-bye
But you are just sleeping
Please, please wake up!
There are hundreds of people here
They want to hear your voice
See your smile

Feel your hugs
We put treasures in the casket with you
Wrote down our regrets, put them in with you
They will be with you, burn with you
Be gone with you
Please, please stop time unfolding
We close the casket
Drive you to the crematorium
Please, please stop time unfolding
We roll the casket into the hot burning box
The door closes
Please, please stop time unfolding
We push the button, the cremation begins
Please, please stop time unfolding
But, NO! it is not possible to stop time
Not possible to create order
It cannot be done
If there is a God, He is in the disorder, is in the heartbreak
This cannot be
Why? Why? Why? Silence. Silence. Silence
They say God is in the silence
God is in the light
And so
I wait in the silence
Wait for light
Wait for transformation
Wait for grace
Wait for spring
I know it will come
I will arrive again
I will be home
There will be beginning again

The force of love will return . . . will return
Because time
Time will not stop unfolding

The Storm

There was a night not long ago
The ground was crumbling beneath me
There was no path to walk
The storm came quickly
Rain, wind, thunder, lightning
And this storm
It was not just all around me
It was in me
I was desperate, needing something to hold onto
It seems in times like these
The ground is the only place to be
It pulls you to your knees
Just let yourself go
I found a rock, a rock I had dragged to my yard in the
    pouring rain
There, you are home I told the rock
I told myself
Hug the rock
You have something to hold onto
Somewhere to rest
Until the storm passes
Until you feel strong again
Until you find your way
Until you are not lost
And the path is clear again

When Words Are Not Enough

There are times in our lives
When words will not come
When words are not enough
When we're too tired to think anyway
Too tired to talk
Then it is time to treat ourselves with tenderness
To protect ourselves
To give ourselves time to gather our resources
Our strength
Our purpose
Our light
And then come gently out of the darkness
Bringing our light
And sharing it with others
Who have been to the darkness
Who go to the darkness still

Beauty Will Save Us

There is a quote I read
"It is beauty that will save us in the end"*
And I believe this with all my heart
The beauty of a gentle touch
Of the one who listens
The beauty of each flower, each tree, each raindrop
Each blade of grass, each rock that stands guard over our
    Mother Earth
There is a place I go
In a field
Where my son's body once laid
And I see the beauty there
Of the ground that held him tenderly
Until the sun did rise
And bathed his darkness with light
Bringing him help
Bringing him gentle hands to hold him
To protect him
To keep him safe from anymore harm
I go to this place, am pulled to the ground,
Am close to him in this place
And I kiss the place where he laid
Because this too is beauty
This too is sacred

Held by Mother Earth

Lately
It feels like the only place to be held
Really held
Is by allowing the earth to hold me close
I can breathe there
I can cry
I can let my heart open
It bleeds
The earth soaks up the blood and the tears
Heals the wound
Ever so gently
Holds my aching body
Until I become calm again
And the earth opens
Releasing the pain
Letting it go
Transforming it into something good and nourishing
Allowing something else to grow
Allowing something else to bloom

Asking Denial to Stay a While

I feel the fog lifting from my mind
I invite denial to stay with me
Offer it tea and biscuits
Keep it busy
No need for it to tell me what I already know
What I do not need to hear
What I cannot be with right now
I keep denial close at hand
Ready to say, to yell if someone comes too close
If the truth comes too close
NO, NO, NO
My mind does not want the truth
It is enough that my heart holds the truth
And it is wide open
Bleeding . . .

Go There . . . to the Ground

Yesterday
The pain was so raw
Unbearable, impossible
I found myself lying on the ground
A soft pillow under my head
A blanket keeping me warm
When invited to the ground, pulled to the ground
Go there
Go there . . .
It is the only place to be
With tears, so many tears
Listening to a soft voice
Telling me there was nothing else I could have done
My son was going to do what he did
He couldn't help it
Couldn't stay
He had to go
This world was too harsh for him
But now
Now what?
We are left to mourn
To yearn for his warm hugs, his smiles, his talks
And ask why, why, why?
Why did you go away?

Living Life as You Find It

There is a quote of Megan Scribner
That goes like this
"I'm only lost if I'm going someplace in particular"
And this seemed so comforting to me
If I could just let go of all my plans
All my expectations of myself and others
All my shoulds and shouldn'ts
Just let life happen
Especially when things have fallen apart
When there are no answers
When the way is no longer clear
Begin to wonder
Let things happen one possibility at a time
One thing leading to the next
You will find your way
And know you were never really lost
You were just living life
As you found it
As it found you

What Waits for Us

Finding our way is sometimes
Just to live it
To know what comes next
Is to do it
The only way to know what waits
Is to wait
To keep going through the motions
One day at a time
One moment at a time
And then there will come a day
When the path has become clear
The ground beneath our feet is firm again
The sun is rising in the east
There is light in the darkness
There is light

Needing to Slow Down

I need to slow down
I'm so tired
Still asking the same questions
Why?
What could I have done?
My heart is so heavy
My whole body aches
I cry
What else is there to do?
A cloud keeps descending on me
I lie down
I cry
I ask the same questions again
There are no answers
I'm so tired
So tired

What Else Is There?

A heaviness has descended on me
An unbearable sadness
The questions still haunting me
Will life ever be okay again?
Someone please tell me this is not happening
My son did not choose death
That could not be
He would not do this
He would not
Oh! The uncertainty, the sorrow
It keeps pulling me to the ground
The only place where there is calm
Where there is stillness, quiet
Being held by Mother Earth
I cry
Tell me he knew he was loved
Tell me it is not true
That it is a dream, a nightmare
That he was not in pain
Tell him I love him
Tell him I am so sorry that he couldn't see past his pain
That we couldn't help him
Tell him that we love him
That's all
For what else is there?
What else is there?

So Much Time

There are times
So many times
It feels like I'm falling apart
Splitting
Watching as I go through the motions
The pain so deep within my body
I don't know what to do
I took one of his shirts last night
I wanted to hold it, wear it
I couldn't do it
I told Chris I was sorry
I cried, I cried
I couldn't do it
Everything hit me so hard
So many emotions
Shaking all over
I threw up
I just couldn't do it
The truth was too close
And it was a truth I couldn't bear
It will take more time
To be with the truth
So much time to find acceptance
So much time
Will there ever be enough time?

So Many Questions

It is so hard to understand
When someone has left
Taken their own life
And taken their secrets with them
Leaving behind questions
So many questions
The things left unsaid
Haunting your every thought
The things left undone
Tearing at the edge of your reality
Why? Why? Why?
How can it be?
Your mind and body and spirit
In so much pain
You didn't know you could survive such pain
And people tell you you'll be okay
You'll survive, maybe thrive
But now
Right now
It is all you can do to breathe
It is all you can do to stay

One Love

I don't understand sometimes
When people think they have to be right
And in being right
They "win"
Meaning of course
That someone else is wrong
Someone else "loses"
There is no way for peace
This way
For the way of peace
Is the way of the heart
And in the way of the heart
There is no right or wrong
There is only love
The one love

In the Shadows

I miss my son so much
It hurts when I allow the truth in
When light shines on the words in my head
"He shot himself!"
He would not do that
I know he would not do that
I cannot think
I cannot breathe
The walls of protection come tumbling down
There is nowhere to hide
The pain in my body is unbearable
It feels impossible to hold on
And then
It is gone
The truth recedes to some dark corner of my mind
I can breathe
I can think
He is just away
And I am in the dark unknown
In the silence that surrounds the answers
In the shadows that hold the questions
So many questions

Broken

There are times I am on my knees
Begging to rewrite the story
Write a different ending
Where my son is alive and happy
A lawyer, married with babies and a puppy
There are times I am lying curled up on the floor
Crying endlessly
Knowing the ending of his story
Knowing I cannot live with it
That it cannot possibly be true
But then there is the truth
The unbearable, impossible truth
That threatens my being
I throw up
I can't breathe
But then something happens
Something inside me changes
And I begin to stand up again
Begin to breathe
Begin to go on with life again
Life as it is
Broken and beautiful
Broken and real
Broken and healing

The Rest of the Way Home

Today the waves of emotion are more gentle
Not pounding in anger at the shore
But rolling in quietly, gently
Still with strength and power
But calm, with ease
For the first time
I held a precious belonging of Chris's
Held his Buddha close to my heart
Felt its calming spirit
The tears fell quietly like a gentle rain
My heart open to any trace of his spirit that might
     still be there
The questions, the confusion still there too
But with gentleness
No anger, no restlessness today
Just gentle, quiet tears
The heart broken open
No more resistance
No more fight
Surrender
And wondering, just wondering
Feeling lost yes, but not in a panic
Just wondering
Watching and waiting
For the path will appear
The one that will take me
The rest of the way home

Being Okay

I was wondering today
If Chris is okay
That's all I want to know
That he's okay
But then I think how did this happen
Why did this happen
It could not have happened
He is just away
Gone to school
Off with his friends
He's fine
Just give me one of your big bear hugs
Let me feel you holding me
Squeezing me
Let me hear the words
I love you Mom
Let me say the words
One more time
I love you Chris
We all love you
We miss you
We want you to come home
We want you to be okay

Show Up like a Rose

I've been taking rose petals with me lately
I scatter them
Over the place where the blood soaked into the earth
Let their beauty cover that place of death
Let them open and rest
Wishing I could do the same
Show up like a rose
Open and full of beauty
Even in this place of death
Open and able to rest
Even here
Where sadness and desperation took a life
Wounded the earth
Wounded the hearts of all who are left
Left to remember
To remember his beautiful smile
His warm hugs
His kind words
His being
Being with us

Can Someone Tell Me

They say nothing is lost
That is held in your heart
But can someone tell me the point of having anything in your
    heart
When your heart is breaking open again and again and again?
I prayed most of my life for all beings to be happy, healthy,
    peaceful, safe, and free
And my son, my beautiful, gentle, peaceful son shot himself
    in the head
I prayed most of my life for the healing of all beings, of the
    earth
I prayed for protection, for healing light, for release of
    negative energy
And my son shot himself in the head
Can someone tell me why
Tell me why we go on
Tell me what's the point
Why the grass is green
Why the trees stand tall
Why the skies are blue
Why roses are red
Why is it a beautiful world?
My son still shot himself in the head
He was the one who was loved by so many
Was so popular
Was caring and gentle
Was generous
Protective and strong
He was the one who had so much to give

The one who had so much to live for
And he shot himself in the head
In a field
Alone
So tell me why
And tell me how will love be the way
Why be with the mystery
When you wake up to the sound of your own crying
How can there be peace and harmony
When someone so kind is the victim and the murderer
What's the point of the gift of your wound if your heart has
     turned to stone
How is it that every day is a sacred gift
When your son shot himself
Can someone tell me why
Can someone tell me how to keep the heart open
How to believe that life goes on
How to believe that love is part of this
That love is still the way

His Light

Forgiveness does not always come easily
And yet there are times forgiveness does come so easily
Forgiveness for the one who left
For leaving the way he did
And you simply cannot understand
And you cannot put the pieces together
You cannot know what was in his mind because he did not
    tell you
You cannot know how he felt or why he chose to leave
    because he did not—could not tell you
But leave he did
With no chance for good-bye
With so many questions, so much confusion, darkness,
    sadness
Pain, terrible pain
That was his death
But his life was love and kindness, clarity, light, happiness,
    fearlessness
His life was forgiveness
I choose forgiveness
I choose to remember his life
His happiness, his clarity, his fearlessness
I choose his love and kindness
I hold his light
I forgive
I ask for him to forgive me
For him to be the light

Hold Onto the Light

When I start longing for what no longer is
When I just want my lost love to come home
When I start asking why, why, why
When I start asking how did this happen
When my mind won't let the truth in
Because it couldn't be, it just couldn't be
The emotions become like a tsunami
Wave after wave of the impossible
And I look for anything to hold onto
Some truth that says it's not possible
There's been a mistake
But I can't breathe
And I can't stand
Because the only place to be is in the truth
And the truth is
He is gone
The truth is
There are no answers
The truth is
The ground is no longer solid
The walls are crumbling
The water is deep and treacherous
There is so little to hold onto
But there is light, will always be light
Even in the darkness, there is light
Hold onto the light

Allowing the Confusion

I was walking in the woods today
A familiar place for me
With its trails and signs along the way
But on this day
Nothing seemed familiar
And the farther I walked
The more confused I felt
The trails were covered in yellow leaves
Everywhere I looked, yellow leaves
The fear began to be palpable
My hands shook
My breath came in short puffs
I felt close to crossing the line that defines being crazy
But then I stopped and sat on a log
I allowed the confusion
Closed my eyes
Allowed the darkness
Took one breath at a time
Became grounded again with the trees
Opened my eyes
And asked for guidance
And the path was there
Not as clear as in the past
But clear enough
And I was fearless enough again

Nature's Resting Place

I had found my way to two logs lying in the leaves
Two trees standing beside them
Just close enough to lean against
Just close enough to ground myself
Just enough to keep from falling into a million pieces
The grief I felt pushing me down
Pulling me apart
Breaking my heart
My legs trembling, my hands shaking
I let myself sink to the ground
Nature's resting place I heard someone say
As a gentle touch rested on my shoulder
Letting me know once more
Everything will be all right
Find a place of rest in the middle of things
And you will find
Everything will be all right

It's Not Far

A lady walking the wooded paths today
Stopped me with that look in her eyes
The one that says "I'm lost"
She asked if I knew the paths well
I said I did, fairly well . . .
Where did she need to go?
She asked what path would take her to a place she could find
      her car
Find her way home
It's not far I said
She collapsed with her son by her side
It's not far she repeated, It's not far
Sometimes, that's all you need to know
It's not far to go
Where you will remember
And you'll know where you are

Where Life Becomes a New Life

There are times when we know
Life will never be the same
And when we journey to that place
And say that was before or that was after
We can look back
See what we have lost
Know what we left behind
Know what we surrendered in order to begin again
And this life "after" is a new life
Is a different life
A life after that memory became a part of your life
A part of your story
A part of "that was after"

One with the Darkness

I had a dream last night
I was standing at the edge of the ocean
The waves pounding on the shore
It was barely light
But light enough to see
To see a mermaid bobbing in the water
Far from the shore
Beckoning me to dive into the cold, dark waters
Her smile seemed to say "it's okay"
You'll be all right
There is beauty as well as darkness under the surface
You must see it all
Accept it all
And then there will be no need for fear
For you will know
You can be—
You must be
One with the darkness
To be one with the light

What Makes Us Whole

There are times in the darkness
When all you want is to keep your eyes closed
Stay with the darkness
And that's okay
The light will come
Just as hope will come from despair
And faith will come from doubt
Clarity will come from confusion
Joy will come from sadness
If we wait
One will become the other
The other will become the one
For it is all there
Always
It is just part of who we are
Part of what makes us whole

To Turn Back Time

I wonder how many times
We wish we could turn back the clock
Yearn for another time
When life was happening around us
But we didn't know what was coming
Didn't notice the change in his eyes
Didn't hear his dark thoughts
Didn't see him turning away
Didn't know he would not stay
And so
We wander through our days
Life still happening around us
And we know what is coming
Hours and days and years without him
And yet
He is all around us
Constantly with us
In our thoughts, our dreams, our memories, our yearning
And most of all
In our broken hearts
That will never be whole again
That will always yearn
To turn back time

Never Alone

This journey we take called life
We seem to do it alone so much of the time
But we are together
All one
For we all experience the same pains
The same hurts of a lifetime
Heartbreaks, yearnings, losses, failures
And we feel so alone
And yet we are never alone
We are on the journey alone
But we do it together
And that is when there is peace
When you awaken to the knowing
That all these things that hurt us
All these things that bring us joy
Are happening
Every day
Every hour
Every second
And so we are together
And though we may walk alone
Someone walks beside us
Every step
Every breath

May There Be Light

People ask me
Why go to the place
Where our beloved was found
Lying in the field
Held by Mother Earth
His life's blood
Bleeding into the ground
And I would tell them
It was the last place he was alive
Where I felt his energy
But over time it has changed
As I honored the earth that held him
As I prayed to heal the wounds
As I spoke to my son, to God, to the One, to Love
I found the reason to be there changing
And now when I visit that place
That sacred place
It is to honor the place
Where one of us suffered
Suffered alone in the dark night of the soul
Where he could not find the light
And I pray for all who suffer
That there may be peace
That there may be rest
That there may be light

Holding All That Is

The more I cry
The more I am afraid
Afraid that Chris is slipping away
With each tear, each moan, each day
And yet
The more I allow my tears
The more alive he seems to me
The memories become more clear
The pictures in my head more focused
And so it seems
I must continue to surrender
Continue to let go
If I am to hold him in my heart
If my heart is to hold all that is
All that has been
All that will be

What Now

Some days I feel like running away
But I don't want to leave home
I don't know what I want
And I don't want anyone else telling me
Telling me what to do, what not to do
I just need time
Please give me time
I just need to rest
Please give me rest
But how can I rest
When I realize I couldn't protect my child
Couldn't teach him to be strong
To be brave, to keep going
To stay
Couldn't teach him to wait and rest
That everything would be different in the morning
What now?
What now?

1 Pray He Felt No Pain

Time has stopped
As I look at the medical examiner's report
I go numb again
I am back to the first day
"The manner of death is suicide
The body is a normally developed male
Tattoos of a tiger's face on the left chest
'Hold my own' on the left shoulder
A cross with Respect on the right shoulder
Karma on the right forearm"
Everything was normal
No abnormalities
He was perfect, my child was perfect
But that night
That dark night of the soul
He drank and drank and drank
Blood alcohol .322
He was out of his mind at that moment
In a total fog
Not feeling
Not knowing right from wrong
Good from bad
He was not himself
And then
"A gunshot wound to the head
Manner of death is suicide"
I pray he felt no pain
I pray he felt no pain

Coming from the Heart

So now I know
My home was not always safe
I was in my own denial
My own not knowing what to do
My own weakness
I did not protect my home
Keep it a safe place
The cycle from my childhood kept alive
This is what I carry hidden
Is what I will need to transform
But right now
I am numb
Crushed by the weight of what I have failed to do in my life
Failed to stand by the truth in my heart
But this is "where the healing begins"*
With the sound of walls crashing down
I begin by knowing I am strong
Knowing I am courageous
Knowing I am grounded
No matter what, I am these things
As we all are, for we are one
And coming from the heart
We are strong, we are courageous, we are rooted in the truth
And in love—in so much love

Healing Begins by Tenth Avenue North

A Healing Journey

A peace has descended upon me today
Reminders of our Chris all around
Reminders that he is not here
Not in the way we want him
And yet, I feel him
I trust he is here somehow
With us
In us
Waiting for us
Giving us strength when we need it
This I believe
I know there will always be pain
The pain of his absence
I will use that pain to remind myself
The healing gift I give to others, we all give to others
Is to be present
Truly present
Now
Trusting that that is enough
My heart is full
Wounded yes, but full of the love all around
Holding us up
Guiding our steps through this journey
This journey of healing
Of learning
Of becoming One

Impossible

I lit a candle this morning
Four months since our hearts broke into a million pieces
Four months since the impossible happened
We ask ourselves sometimes
How did we miss it?
But we did not miss it
We have to let go of that idea
It was beyond our ability to comprehend
We could never have seen it coming
It was the impossible
How on earth did we get here
Where we have a memory tree in the park
We attend candle lighting services
We create a time capsule
We have his ashes on my altar
It is not possible
And yet
Here I sit
Lighting a candle at three in the morning
A new heaviness with every breath
My heart bleeding out slowly
The sounds of emptiness all around
For he is not coming home
He took his own life . . . impossible

To Follow the Heart

For any of us to heal
It seems we have to follow the heart
Listen to the body
Stay connected to the soul
So that
When you need to rest, you rest
When you need to cry out to the heavens, you cry out
When you need to weep, you allow the tears to flow
When you need to hold on, you hold on
When you need to let go, you let go
And you keep listening to your inner guide
Your inner wisdom
Your heart
Follow where it leads
And it will lead you where you need to be
Will lead your heart to healing
To peace within
To love

Staying in Time with Time

I want to sleep
I want to dream
To take a break
And not wake up
Until this nightmare is over
But time keeps carrying us forward
Like a river that keeps flowing
The days keep slipping by
Time, relentless time, marching on
As if this hasn't happened
As if nothing has changed
And yet
Every day is another day without Chris
And maybe—maybe another day to heal
The rest of us together
Taking turns
We light a candle for Chris
We decorate the Christmas tree
We carry on
What choice do we have
We have to keep moving
Staying in time with time
It slows down for no one
The days keep slipping by
Darkness, light, darkness, light
Maybe one day, we can stay with the light

You Live a Life

I never understood before
That "you don't choose a life,
You live a life"*
Until now
Life has happened
We have lost someone so dear to us
We must learn to live this life
This life of darkness for now
To live it feels like I must find a warm, safe place to be
I long to just be
I yearn to go inward and heal
It is such hard work to be okay
To let go
The urge to hold on is so strong
But with each teardrop
That flows down my cheek
There is hope
Hope for finding peace
Hope for living this life
Living with purpose and care and joy

*a quote from the movie *The Way*

Lean into the Pain

The only way I know to learn, to grow, to change from this
    heaviness in my heart
This impossible pain
Is to lean into it
Invite the pain to teach me
Teach me to see
To find the inner wisdom
That comes from my spirit, my soul
To find the wisdom that comes from the All
From the One
From Love

He Will Stay in My Life

With the intention to heal in my heart and mind
I know it will not be easy
There is work to do
To keep my beloved in my life and to let him go
But somehow
He will stay in my life
Be my teacher, my guide
He will not drain my life
He will give me life
As he did when I hugged him in the coffin
His life entered me
And I was calm beyond any reason, beyond any
    understanding
I just know he is a part of me
Always in my heart, body, and mind
Together we will go forward
Giving back to life
Giving back to love

Finding Courage

The waves of sadness and tears feel unbearable at times
You think this can't go on
But it keeps coming
Wave after wave of unbelievable pain
You think this can't be real
But you know it is
The temptation to stop trying is strong
You think you want to die
But you find the will and courage to keep going
And you do normal things
Always on guard
Fearing you might collapse
But you find a place of stillness inside
And you see that life is precious still
Even with this
Even with this

I Surrender

I am filled with a new resolve
To heal body and mind and soul
And to heal I am told
I have to let go of having to know why
Have to trust in a higher power
In a universal destiny
And let go
And so here I stand
I surrender
Again and again and again

The Breath

It seems the only way to let go
Let go of all the questions
Let go of the pain, the unbearable pain
Is to let it out through the body
To yell, to scream
To cry
To breathe
Let it all out through the breath
Take in what is good through the breath
Let go of what is bad through the breath
And then we get up again
Try again to live
Live a life of purpose
Live a life on purpose
Find peace
Be peace
Until it is time
To let go again
To let the breath
Do its healing work again

In Our Dreams

I sit and write Christmas cards
Something so normal to do
And yet it does not feel normal at all
My chest is heavy
I just can't believe
Chris, our Christmas baby, is not coming home
Everyone says how happy he was
How funny, how smart
How important his friends and family were
But somehow he chose to leave
And we are left
With heavy hearts
Going through the motions
Sadness upon sadness
But I hope he sees more than the sadness
I hope he sees how much he was loved
Sees how much he is missed
Sees we will keep him in our hearts
In our lives
In our dreams

Life Goes On

With sadness so profound
The tears fall gently down my cheeks
The emptiness so complete
The heaviness of the heart suffocating
So difficult to catch my breath
Memories flooding my mind
And then the grace that comes
For no apparent reason
Hope fills my soul
Forgiveness overflows my heart
Trust tells me there is a bigger picture
Trust tells me things are as they are meant to be
Life goes on
Life goes on

A Place to Hold On

A place to hold on
This is a place of transition
A place filled with possibilities
A place of healing
A place of love
Where am I?
I am where I need to be
Shining light on the darkness
A place of surrendering to what is
A place where confusion becomes clarity
A place where sadness and grief become courage
Where fear becomes trust
Where anger becomes kindness
Where impatience becomes warmth
Where worry becomes being present
This is a place of transition
A place filled with possibilities
A place of healing
A place of love
Where am I?
I am here
Beginning again
Eyes wide open
Heart melting
Spirit going with the flow
Ready to learn, to change, to grow

If I Could See You

It's amazing how we keep going
Even when the heart is broken into a million pieces
People have no idea what is happening behind your face
And do we see what's behind theirs?
What if we could see each other
Glimpse what was really happening
What if we could really say "I see you" and mean it
What then?
What then?

Life Keeps Moving Along

Life is always moving along
Sometimes, it seems, faster than other times
But it is really the same
It depends on what we notice
And I wonder, what have I missed along the way?
What glance?
What sigh?
What change?
And what difference would it make
Perhaps the difference between hope and despair?
Between doubt and faith
Between joy and sadness
Between light and darkness
Is it possible to see?
To really see
To make a difference
To make time slow down
To have another chance
To notice
To make a different choice
Before life keeps moving along
And the story has changed
Changed to a story that never should have been?

Every Breath

One thing that can happen
When someone leaves you bereft
Leaves you suddenly
With no warning
At least, no warning that you knew about
One thing that can happen
Is your life changes
Your purpose changes
Over time you start to see it
You have a new job
And that job keeps you going
Gives you a reason to get up in the morning
To keep putting one foot in front of the other
To breathe
Gives you a purpose
To live your life with hope
With love, with trust
Trust that life is precious
Life is beautiful
Life is worth every breath

Going through the Motions

It's Christmas Eve
How do you get through the holidays
With something so impossible on your thoughts
In your heart?
I just go through the motions
Numb inside
No words
Just watching myself do what I've done for so many years
     before
Make the special dinner
Make the special brownies
Pretend the unthinkable hasn't happened
Pretend life goes on
Keep going through the motions
And maybe
One day
The impossible will be just a memory
A memory that no longer takes my breath away
A memory that brings with it the goodness of who he was
That brings with it the seeds of life
The seeds that have grown since
The impossible happened

What Holds Us Together

I want time to slow down sometimes
Just for a little while
Just let me catch my breath
Just so I can bless all the beauty in our lives
Not forget
That life is good
Not forget
What holds us together
The love between us
The stories between us
But time keeps marching on
Like there is somewhere to go
Something to do
And really . . .
There is nowhere to go
Nothing to do
Just be with love
Be with the ones we love
Be with what holds us together

Our Hope

We keep him with us
Carrying him in our hearts
We let him go
With every tear that flows
And we hope
That like the words of the song
"In the arms of the angels
He may find some comfort there"*
And when we look up in the sky
Sometimes we see through our tears
A cloud that looks like an angel
And we hope
Maybe it's him
Letting us know he's okay
Letting us know
He's at peace
That is our hope always
That he is at peace

Angel by Sarah McLachlan

The Depths of Grief

When you are in the depths of grief
You have to live through the heart
You have to do what feels right to do
Cry, cry, and cry some more
Go somewhere safe
Hold onto something solid
For me, holding onto a rock felt comforting
Telling Chris over and over again
How sorry I was that this happened to him
That he had so much pain
And we didn't know
That he had so much pain
He took his own life
And so now
I hurt
My whole body hurts
And I have to cry
Release the tears
Ask my questions
Want him back
Let him go

Being Grateful

We have to remind ourselves
Of all the beauty that remains
That this life is precious
Worth fighting for
My body is working hard right now
Feeling so many feelings
It's hard work
And so
I must take care of my body
No more eating cookies and fudge all day
Though they bring some comfort
I have to trust that somehow we'll get through this
Together
Body, mind, and spirit
Taking care
Noticing the beauty all around
Being grateful for what is left
Being grateful for what is left

A Little Letting Go

I decided to stop going to the field
To stop visiting the place where Chris took his life
The place where the earth was wounded
I walked to it for the last time
I sang "Amazing Grace"
Spread rose petals on the snow
Saw how the memory of our footsteps would always be there
Coming from our house, down the street
Around the corner and across the field
Back around to our house
Our footsteps making the shape of a heart in the snow
Over and over and over again
Connecting us through time and space
I left with a sense of peace, amazing grace
Saying good-bye, allowing for a little letting go
And then a miracle of sorts—it snowed six inches that day
Nine more the next day
The field covered in a pure white blanket
No more footsteps, no more wounded earth
Sleeping at last, waiting for spring, waiting for new life

To Sleep

Sleep, sweet sleep
I slept last night
So peaceful this morning
No tears
Reminding myself I am not abandoning my child
I am learning to love him and hold him in a different way
I am learning ways to honor him without falling apart
Letting go little by little
Grateful for any healing
With tears
Without tears
Trusting
As life goes on
Trusting the process
Trusting Chris
Trusting the Universe
Trusting myself
Breathing the sweet air
Allowing sweet sleep

When Death Comes

When death comes in the night
Suddenly
Unexpectedly
You discover how deep your love is
And the depth of your love
Matches the depth of your pain
So deep
So deep
And the questions that haunt you
But if you can open your heart
Sometimes you will see someone who looks like him
You'll hear his laugh
A sweet memory will pass by your eyes
You'll "see" him
And you know
This will help you through another day
Even though you still ask
"Oh, how can this be?"

Surrender

The earth opens—a sprout appears
A bud opens—a flower appears
A tree reaches for the sky
Its branches open
A womb opens
A baby is born
The clouds blow by
The sun appears
A wave crashes on the shore
Returns to the sea
Comes back to crash on the shore again
The heart opens
We let go
Peace and calm

No-Man's Land

You find yourself in a no-man's land
When someone you love
Has taken his own life
The questions are endless
Ones impossible to answer
Why? How? Who knows what happened?
And this no-man's land turns into a swamp
You never know when you will slip and fall
When the quicksand will take you down
When you won't be able to breathe
And then there are the voices
Asking you why you didn't do more
What did you miss
What went so wrong
And you feel so alone in this no-man's land
But then you summon the courage
And you open your eyes
And you see there are so many others
Struggling and suffering with the same unfinished story
And you hold each other up
You have to, to get to the other side
You show each other the goodness
The beauty
The footsteps to follow
The memories so sweet
Remind each other of the reasons to go on, of all that was and
    is right
Of the ways to keep loving the one who is lost
While letting him go

Ways to hold him in a safe place
A place in your heart
While you climb out of this no-man's land
And one day, somewhere on this path
You will find a way to begin again

Crazy Days

Some days are just crazy days
As you dive to the depths of your knowing
You find debris from days gone by
And oh! How you want to change something
Heal something, change course
So you don't find yourself in this place of ultimate humility
    and loss
So your path does not lead to this "perfect storm"
Where everything has gone wrong
You don't know who you are anymore
Don't know what you believe
Or what purpose your life has
And so you have crazy days
Tears that won't stop falling
Angry voices in your head
Unbelievable hurt in your heart and spirit
And all you can do is breathe
And wait
Wait for this storm to pass
For the sun to set on this crazy day
So that you can find a place to rest
And a new path, a place to begin again
Tomorrow

Love Is the Dance

It is said that life is a dance between life and death
That we are each responsible for our own dance
Our own story
And to honor another's story
We must give them the gift of their story
To give them the choice to create their own story
To be responsible for their life
And for their death
And if they have chosen death
Honor that
Let them go
While honoring their life
Honoring what they meant to us
Holding them close
And surrendering to their story
Remembering their goodness
Forgiving their mistakes
Allowing for the possibility
That this was meant to be
In the bigger picture
There was a destiny
That we cannot see
Cannot understand
But can honor
Because we are one
We are love
And love
Is everything
Love is the dance
The dance between life and death

In the Pain

It is said that even the deepest pain will pass
That there will always be light in the darkness
And just as sometimes the stars are hidden
They will shine through
The moon will glow and guide your eyes upward
And the beauty of the night
Is the darkness
With the light shining through
Reminding you
There is beauty still
Even in the darkness
There is somewhere to look for hope
Somewhere to look for beauty
Even in the darkness
Even in the pain

Change Will Come

All of our lives have some chaos, some calm
Things that create change
Things that make room for new possibilities
New beginnings
So that there is always a chance for balance
The storms in our lives create waves to wash away the debris
Create winds to blow away the old
And so
When we are in the middle of the storm
We need to find something solid to hold onto
A rock, a belief, a value, a faith
That will keep us grounded
As the winds blow
As the rain falls
And then there will be calm again
And as we welcome spring after a long, hard winter
We will welcome the calm of our lives
A place to rest
A place to surrender
A place to begin again

Why

There are times lately
When I cannot feel any sense of Chris
I am numb again
And wonder
Was he really here
Or did I make him up
Was he always a fantasy
Or is this life now a fantasy
I don't know what's real anymore
What can I trust
When nothing makes sense anymore
There is just life and death
Both so random
When nothing makes sense
Does anything matter
Do we have a purpose
Are we meant to be here
When why is the only question
Why is he gone
Why am I here
Why is anyone here
But then I think
There has to be a reason
A purpose
There was a reason he was here
He was love
He was light in the darkness
His life was a gift
His memory is a gift

Another Chance

I understand now
Why people make deals with the devil
For I found myself this morning
Begging for some way to bring him back
There must be a way I cried
It was a mistake, an accident
Just bring him back
I'd do anything
And not just me
All of us who love him
If there were some way to bring him home
We would do it
Make a deal
Give up our own lives
But there are no deals to be made
Only memories to hold onto
Maybe some purpose or meaning to find
A reason to go on, to let him go
But right now
I'd rather make a deal with the devil
Or with God if he'd make one
To give him another chance at life
To give us another chance to hold him
To love him
To keep him close

Seeing the Truth

When someone takes their own life
I guess we all have to ask at some point
Why?
Maybe not
But it seems there comes a day
When you have to look at what you missed
And it is painful, so painful
Because you have to know
Not everyone who attempts suicide
Is successful
So why our beloved?
And you see the truth
There were times you didn't see him clearly
Didn't hear what he tried to tell you
Weren't there in the way he needed you
Weren't there in the way he needed you
You were not enough
But you have to be humbled
You have to cry those tears
Not tears of blame or guilt
But tears of sorrow and forgiveness
Forgiving yourself
Because you must also see the truth
There was nothing you could do
No matter your good intentions
You can't control what someone else does
Everyone is the captain of their own ship
A ship powered by their own thoughts, emotions,
    and imagination

You can't save them from themselves
You just love them
You can't read their minds
Or see into their hearts
You can only trust
Trust that this was their story
Trust that they are okay

All One

If we are to live
If we are to thrive
It seems we must know
We must feel
How deeply we are connected to all things
For without the connections
We are afloat
Drifting as if in outer space
So far away, we imagine
From what we need
From who we are
Separated from love
Even though the love is all around
Separated
And when we are separated from love
We are separated from life
From the life force
And that is when darkness blinds our way
We stumble, we fall
And perhaps
We cannot get up
No second chance
We have drifted too far
The fog is too thick
We are lost
Lost in our own mind
Disconnected from the heart
And in a moment of carelessness
Gone from this world

Gone with the mystery
Gone back to love, to the One
To the All

Go Within

I think I know how I might heal this time
I keep going through the fog
One step at a time
Opening my eyes from time to time
Looking to see if there is anything familiar
Closing my eyes, I go within
As the waves of grief crash through
Reminding myself to breathe
Reminding myself not to resist
Let it push and pull me as it will
Let it wash the debris away
And as the waves recede, let myself rest
Going with the flow
Open my eyes again
See what has changed
See what has washed away
See what is still here
Reflect
Do I need to let more go?
Does anything feel familiar?
Does anything feel right?
Is there something to hold onto?
Close my eyes again, go within
Rest
Wait
Hold on
Let go
Keep going
One day at a time

Where Did You Go My Love?

Where did you go my love?
To some dark, dark place
That swallowed you up
Left you confused, scared, despairing, and lost
And in that place
You could not find home, could not find the light
And though you spoke of love
You forgot that you were loved
And for a moment
Just a moment
You thought life was not worth the fight
And you were gone
With a mistake, an accident
With the flash of a bullet
You fell to the ground
Held by Mother Earth
Guarded by the trees standing there
I'm sure they were bereft
Feeling your pain
Soaking up your blood
And in the same moment
My prayer, my hope is that the angels lifted you up
Took you to the light
Kept you there
Held you close
Where you were safe
Where you know you are loved
No more pain
No more darkness

No more separation
You are found
You are home
But where did you go my love?
For now we cannot find home
Cannot find the light
We are in the darkness
We are lost without you

Coming Home

When you lose someone so near to your heart
Your heart feels heavy and empty at the same time
Heavy with sorrow and the pain of loss
Empty with hunger for their touch
For the sound of their voice
For that special smile
But as time passes by
And you learn to trust what you cannot see
Cannot hear
Cannot feel
You learn that there is room in your heart
That nothing is lost
You can find comfort in the memories
Comfort in the things you did do
And you learn
That even in this pain
There is a teacher
Is a message
There is love
There is being found
There is coming home

Life without Him

Sometimes I am afraid
That life without him will always feel this way
That my heart will always be heavy
That my mind will always be confused, doubtful,
    and despairing
That I will be frightened by the sound of the phone
That I will be anxious every time someone is late
That I will not know who I am
Or what my purpose is
But life is not like that
Time keeps moving on
Life changes
Your heart begins to soften
Your mind seeks clarity and hope
You learn to let things go
You find what there is to hold onto
And with time
With this never-ending movement of time
Harmony returns
Balance returns
Life goes on . . .

The Wind Keeps Blowing

Sometimes it still feels like I cannot breathe
It's been nearly six months
But still I can't believe it's true
Can't believe we'll never see him again
There are days I wake up crying
Days I go to bed crying
And as I look out my window
The wind blowing
The snow falling steadily
Inches upon inches upon inches
I think of the wisdom of the polar bear
Of the healing power of going within
Seeking out the darkness
And waiting
Waiting for something to give birth
Something that will bring hope and faith
Something that will bring joy into this sadness
Something that will bring light into this darkness
And I know it will come
There will be a birth
There always is
There will be a spring
There always is
It is the way of life
And death
The wind will keep blowing, there will be life again

Sealed in My Heart

Some days
I see pictures of him
Flashing through my mind
Pictures of the boy he was
And of the young man he became
Pictures of times with friends and family and pets
Times of happiness, contentment, love,
     and times of heartbreak
Good times, bad times, good times again
Life the way it was
The way it is
And it is good to know
These pictures, these memories
Are sealed away in my heart
A place where they will never be lost
Where he will never be lost

What If

Six months ago today
Was the last day our beloved was alive
And I wonder
Did he know what he was going to do?
Was he thinking about it all day?
Was he happy that day with his friends?
They all say he was
He walked the dog
He went for a swim
He played golf
Got a haircut
He texted with friends
He was with friends all day and into the night
Never uttered a word of distress
Nor a thought that life was too much for him
It wasn't until two in the morning
Things seem to have unraveled
Everyone else was asleep
He had another drink
The darkness must have gathered around him
What if I had called him?
What if anyone had called him?
What if he had just passed out?
What if . . . what if . . . what if . . .
There is nowhere to go with what if . . .
We cannot change the ending
No matter how many what ifs we think of
We can only be with what is
As impossible as it seems

It is done
The ending to one story has been written
There is something waiting to be born that will
    change everything
Something that will bring light into the darkness
And so . . . I wait . . . I wait

Letting Him Go

I don't know why I dreaded this day
The day that marks six months of death
I didn't dread other days
Ones you would think would be harder
Thanksgiving, Christmas, his birthday, New Years
All floated by
No more painful than the days before
No less painful than the days before
But this day
This day of death
Is tearing me apart
I can see him so clearly
And yet behind a veil
And this is the day I let him go
I asked for his love and forgiveness
Asked him to bless my staying in the world
Asked him to bless my work in the world
And most of all I asked for him to bless me as his mom
That I was enough
I thanked him for being who he was in the world
I blessed him with love and forgiveness
I blessed his leaving
Prayed for his peace and happiness
Prayed that he was at rest
And then with my heart breaking open,
I sent him a kiss good-bye
And let him go
Let him go to love and light
Let him go home
At least
For today

Only Truth

I've promised myself to get up early in the mornings
Rise with the sunrise
Wake up to appreciate another day
Be grateful
But today
I just couldn't make myself do it
I just laid there
No thoughts
No feelings
Just wanting to wait
Wanting to stop and rest
Because letting go is splitting me apart
I know you have to let go to heal
And I know letting go is not abandonment
Is not betrayal
It still feels like it
Feels like guilt
Guilt is a huge demon to overcome
I want to cleanse myself of guilt
It is not truth
I want only truth in my life
Truth
Only truth
And truth says letting go is healing
Letting go is still loving him
Letting go is loving myself and others too
Letting go is sealing him away in my heart
Holding him there
But my God

Dear God
This is hard
So very, very hard

Paradox

It's hard to explain what is happening
The changes to my heart, mind, and spirit
There is a kind of sad acceptance
A calm that settles over me from time to time
Accepting that I must let him go
Release him and yet hold him in my heart
Hold him in this different way
Hold him this way
As life goes on
I must keep going with life
I am still of this world
Still need to take care of myself and others
All the while honoring him
Remembering him
Because his leaving has left a huge hole in my heart
And in my life
And yet
I am still whole
My life, my heart still full
Paradox on paradox on paradox
This is life
Being whole while carrying such woundedness
It is as they say
That "the wound is the place where the light enters you"

Life Is a Gift

I have heard it said
Joy and pain can live—should live in the same house
That one does not eliminate the other
And it is true
Though there are days of great sadness
When one of you has left
Leaving the others with broken hearts and questions that
cannot be answered
But there is joy too
Gratitude for the memories
Gratitude for life as it is
With the sounds of children making plans
Their voices filled with excitement
The soft sharing between partners and friends
The sound of the wind, the rain, the water
The warmth of the sun, the earth, the moon
The changing of the seasons
Both in nature and in ourselves
Life goes on
Life is a gift
One with sadness
One with joy

Do What You Can

When you have faced your worst nightmare
Accepted life as it is
With its pain and sorrow
With its loss
There is not much you can't do
Nothing left to fear
When what you feared most
Has happened
Has come true
When you let it break your heart open
Something shifts inside of you
You see the world through a different lens
You see the world as it is
Wounded
Hurting
Longing to be loved
Longing to be one
And you know
You must do what you can do
To bring hope to where you are
To bring connection
To bring wholeness

The Long, Cold Winter

Everyone seems to be getting tired of wintertime
The snow, the ice, the cold
But this morning
As I walked my dog
It seemed like a winter wonderland
And I found myself feeling grateful
For the beauty of it all
The frosted trees
The blue, blue skies
The sunshine
The glistening snow
The fairy dust floating all around
It was still beautiful
Still something to be grateful for
For it is life
And life . . .
Life is precious . . .
Worth every moment
Every snowflake
Every ray of sunshine
Even in the long, cold winter
Life is beautiful

Wave upon Wave

The sadness of this grief keeps coming wave upon wave
    upon wave
The body's pain so deep
The feeling of stones in the stomach
Of such heaviness on the heart
Such yearning to see, to hear, to feel a presence that is
    gone forever
The feelings of absence
Fill you with such darkness
An aching comes over you
Like a huge wave
Churning up every question
So many questions
And memories
Memories of times you made mistakes
And then the wave recedes
Taking with it
The unanswered questions
And you rest
For a little bit
Until the next wave
Comes and goes
And so it is
And so it is

A Sweet Good-bye

You came to me in a dream last night
You filled me with peace
Such gentleness
Such sweetness
Just a hug
A big bear hug
Like you used to give
And the words
"I love you"
I felt you in my arms
And me in yours
And then you were gone
But oh such compassion I felt
I could only be grateful
For your having been there
And then I knew
It was our good-bye
The one we didn't have time for
But now
It is complete
We had good-bye
Such a gentle, sweet good-bye

Accept It All

To live through a crisis
And come through to the other side
Fully alive
You have to surrender it seems
To the struggle
To the fear
To the judgments
Your own and others
Accept it all
Even the resistance
For in the acceptance
Is freedom
Freedom to forgive yourself
Freedom to breathe again
Freedom to go with the flow
To keep living
One day at a time
One moment at a time
Until one day you can say
"The wound is where the light came in"

It Will Always Change

And so it is with many of us
There is something in us
That is often yearning
For something else
Yearning for possibilities, for movement, for change perhaps
Yearning for truth, for answers, for rest
We perhaps experience one thing and then we know we want
    the other
So that in a lie we want truth
In confusion we want clarity
In busyness we want peace
When we are at home
We want to be away
When we are away
We want to be home
So what is the answer
How do we find a balance?
Experience harmony within?
We stay in the present moment
Accept it as it is
Breathe it in
And then it will always change

Hope

I never really understood
The line of Emily Dickinson's poem
"Hope is the thing with feathers"
But then this morning
Standing on the icy sidewalk
Huddled in my heavy winter coat
The cold wind blowing around me
In a moment of grace
A tiny white feather appeared from nowhere
It floated gracefully on the breeze
Up, down, around, and up again
And as suddenly as it had appeared
It disappeared
It felt magical
Surrounded with mystery
It felt like something was there
Just checking in
Just letting me know
Everything is all right
Everything is all right

Some Day

It is like being frozen in motion
When you are working your way through grief
You keep putting one foot in front of the other
Not knowing how you are doing it
Not really feeling
Not really knowing where you are going
But you keep going
Keep getting up
Looking around
Though nothing looks familiar
Keep going forward
Though what you yearn for
Is not there
You keep going
Because you know
That life is worth living
And some day
You'll find your way back
To being alive
To moving with the flow
To feeling again

Feel the Wind on Your Face

It's a hard road to walk
When everything seems unfamiliar
When you don't recognize your life anymore
Because
For whatever reason
A force as strong as a tsunami
Has moved through your being
And you are stunned
You are all but immobilized
But the wind keeps blowing
And ever so gradually
You start to feel again
Feel the wind upon your face
Feel yourself taking deep breaths
You begin to move
Picking up the pieces
Leaving behind what doesn't belong anymore
Creating something new
Beginning again
And all the while
The wind keeps blowing

That Place of Gratitude

Pain is a good teacher
Though we often resist its lessons
It can open up your heart
It can show you what you need to accept
Show you what needs forgiving
Even when what you need to forgive
Is yourself
Because nothing anyone else does
Is within your control
Because we cannot change
What someone else has done
We can only learn to live with it
Accept it
Learn from it
Find where the gratitude is
And learn to live from that place
Live through that place
That place
Of gratitude

I Thank Him

It's been seven months as I write this
Seven months since the unthinkable happened
And as broken as I feel
I want my son to know
I am okay
I don't want him to worry
If there is such a thing as worry in heaven
I want him to know
As much as I miss him
As much as I wish what happened
Never happened
As much as I wish he had stayed
I want him to know
I love him
I forgive him
I thank him for the time he gave us
I thank him for being who he was
For choosing us
For teaching us

Remember

Sometimes I think I'm losing my mind
Thinking about ways I could change the past
If I could just go back seven months
Just seven months!
I could do something differently
I could go back further
Change my life
Change this story
But all I can hope
Is if I come back again
I will remember
It won't happen this way
But gosh
Sometimes I can't even remember now
Remember to stay in the present
Remember that love is all that matters
Maybe the best I can do
When I forget
Is to come back
And remember

Knowing What I Know

Walking my dog this morning
We went by the bus stop
There was a teenager there
Not dressed for the weather
Clearly he was cold
His mom came by
Offered him a coat
He gave her that look teenagers give
That says "you're embarrassing me"
"I'm fine, Mom" he said
With that tone of voice that pleads with you to not do this
His mom, looking hurt, sped away
I cried
For what would I do
To have those days back?
Knowing what I know now
Knowing what I know now

He Didn't Let Us Know

He didn't give me a chance to respond
Didn't give any of us a chance to respond
To the things he was worried about
To the things he struggled with
To his suffering
Because he didn't let us know
Didn't give voice to what worried him
To what he was struggling with
He didn't speak his truth
And so, we couldn't speak back
Couldn't be there for him
Couldn't be with him in that dark night of the soul
Couldn't begin to save him
Or help him to save himself
Because he didn't let us know
Didn't give us a chance
Didn't give himself a chance

Even with This

I've been thinking a lot about healing lately
And what it means to heal
Because I want to heal
I want to use the experiences of my life
Use them as teachers
And a crisis can be a good teacher
Losing my son
Even this
And the pain of it
Is a good teacher
A teacher that tells me to heal
But does not take the pain away
To heal
Means you learn to be compassionate with yourself
With others
With your pain
And little by little
You live your life
Moving forward
Celebrating life
Even with this

Signs of Life

I cry every day
But I know I am healing
Because I laugh every day too
Or at least I smile
I appreciate the sun on my face
The cool breezes
The music on the radio
The laughter next door
The walks with the dogs
The books I read
Time with friends and family
Signs of spring
Signs of life
It is good
It is very good

It Makes No Sense

A friend of my son's
Wrote to me the other day
He misses Chris so much
He knows he never meant to hurt anyone
It doesn't make sense
He was the protector
A strong person
A person who always looked out for friends and family
It doesn't make sense
Some things in life will never make sense
And yet
All you can do is accept them
For if you don't
You will go round and round forever
Forever in the darkness
Forever in confusion
But the way out of darkness
Out of confusion
Is to believe
Believe he is still watching out for us
Still protecting us
Accept that some day
We will understand
But not now
For now it makes no sense
And all we can do
Is accept that
Accept that it makes no sense

Take My Anger

The anger has started bubbling up lately
They say God can take your anger
But what good is that?
What difference does that make?
What kind of God lets these things happen?
Someone takes his life
Someone who needed more time
He needed more time to learn
To grow
To understand things change
He just needed more time
The most precious gift of all
And yet
Time was taken away
Taken away from all of us
And we're supposed to take comfort
In knowing God can take our anger?
Well God
You do that
Take my anger . . .

You Are Just Away

You are just away
That's what I tell myself
When I cannot face the truth
When my body begins to tremble
And my head begins to hurt
When I think I will lose my mind
And there is nowhere to rest
I tell myself
Over and over and over again
You are just away, you are just away, you are just away
And slowly, gradually
I come back to myself
A calm descends over me
And I know
It is true
You are just away

Breathe, Just Breathe

I don't know if this will ever be okay
But right now
My feelings change as often as the weather
From denial to acceptance to denial again
The tears flow
The tears stop
The heaviness comes and goes
Sleep is elusive
The mind constantly wondering
Wondering why this happened
Wondering how this happened
Wondering what to do now
When the only thing to do it seems
Is to keep putting one foot in front of the other
And to breathe
Just breathe

Sometimes

Sometimes
It feels like a piece of me is missing
A part of me is gone
Like having a piece of the puzzle missing
And as much as I look for it
The more I try to find it
I lose other parts of myself
And so
It seems
The work to do now
Is to create a new me
Figure out who I am now
Figure out how to become whole
Even with this missing part
Even with this hole in my heart
There is a place where nothing is lost
And perhaps
If I look there
I will find myself
Find a way to be
Find a way to carry on

All Becomes Quiet

My mind is like a runaway train sometimes
In danger of running off the track
Of plunging into the darkness
The questions come one after another
The confusion overwhelming
For there are no answers
My thoughts spin out of control
My body begins to tremble
I fall to my knees
Unable to stand
I close my eyes
Entering the darkness
Fear my constant companion
And I cry
A river of tears
Until exhausted
My mind becomes calm
Just as the dust settles after a crash
All becomes quiet
All becomes quiet

To Let Go While Holding On

To let go while holding on
This seems to be the work after loss
To struggle with the pain, the sadness, the hurt
With the absence
Which has become so much a part of me
While I know
I need to let go
To be present in my own life
To be with the ones who are here
Who I love just as much
But I don't want to lose him
I want him in my life
To somehow be a presence
Not an absence
To be with me
But not destroying me
Not taking my life too
For I want to live
I want to love
I want to be
And so it seems
I must learn to let go
While holding on
To remember
And sometimes
To forget

Life Is Precious Still

These are difficult days
Impossible sometimes
When waves of sorrow come
It feels so dark
It feels as if you can't breathe
But then the waves recede
You begin to catch your breath
You feel exhausted for a while
But then a little light returns
You can breathe again
And you know
You are alive
And you want to stay
You need to stay
For life is precious still
Life is precious still

Each Day

They say it takes a lot of strength
To pull yourself together
When your life has fallen apart
A lot of courage
To keep standing up and going forward
But I don't feel strong
Nor courageous
I feel as weak as a kitten
And as vulnerable
But each day brings something new
Something to be grateful for
Even if it is a memory
A sweet picture in the mind
Of a life that did have joy
Of a life that did bring joy

How?

I see him sometimes
Just behind my eyelids
With his bright smile
His sparkling eyes
His warm hug
And then a darkness descends
Always with the same question
Why, why, why?
He had so much to live for
So many who loved him
But there must have been a part of him
That he could not love
A part of him
That could not stay
And that part of him
Took all of him away
Leaving us to love him with aching hearts
Trying to understand
How that part of him
Could be so cruel
How that part of him
Could have taken him away

Carry On

As I walked our dog yesterday
We approached an empty truck
The windows down, the doors open wide
The radio playing
The words of the song
Floating across the air
"Mama, I didn't mean to hurt you . . .
If I don't come home tomorrow
Carry on . . . carry on"
I was frozen in place
He was the only one who called me mama
He is the one not coming home
And so
I open my heart
And take it as a message
From the Universe
From Love
From him
He didn't mean to hurt me
He didn't mean to hurt anyone
He wants us to carry on
And now
That is what we must do
Knowing he is with us always
We will carry on, carry on
Somehow, we will carry on

The New Reality

It's Easter Sunday
He should be home
Home with us
Wearing bunny ears
Decorating the bunny cake
Hiding Easter eggs
How could he not be here?
It isn't fair
I hate this "new reality"
It sucks
That's all I have to say
It sucks

Anger

I don't know why
But this terrible anger
Has been bubbling up lately
An anger that makes me want to scream
That makes me feel like I will explode
It feels so scary
So out of control
Like a huge storm
Blowing through my body
The wind howls
Tree branches break
Glass shatters
It's like a tornado
Cars and trucks flying through the air
The rain pounding on the earth
The noise of it unbearable
And then
Gradually, the storm recedes
All becomes quiet
I return to my body, to my breath
I cry gently
I curl up, exhausted
I sleep

Just Breathe

It's hard not to get angry
When something terrible has happened
That is completely out of your control
There is nothing you can do to change it
Nothing
The impossible has happened
And there are no second chances
No way to make it right
No way to change it
So you have to feel the anger too
Scream, cry, hit something, run like crazy
Until it has been released
And you find your way to the terrible hurt
The hurt that runs beneath all anger
Release it in your tears
In your breath
Until you feel yourself soften
Until you can just breathe again
Until you can just breathe

To Stay

Some days
I think
This can't be my life
Every day
The choice I have to make
To get up
To keep going
To try to make a difference
To stay
When some days
It would be so much easier
To pull the covers over my head
Pretend it didn't matter
If I got up or not
But the truth is
It matters
Each one of us matters
And it matters that we stay
That we keep going
And just by staying
We make a difference
I wish he had known
To stay
That's all we need to do
Stay, be who we are
For tomorrow will come and tomorrow matters

Let the Wind Blow

I was walking in the woods yesterday
The weather matched my mood step for step
The sky was dark
The wind was howling
The trees creaking and moaning
Their branches swaying back and forth
And the wind kept blowing
But the trees
They stayed grounded
Though they were blown by the wind
Pelted by the rain
They stayed firmly rooted
Rooted where they were
And I thought
This is the way to walk this path of sorrow
Stay grounded
Feel your feet on the earth
Your heart will keep beating
Your lungs will keep breathing
The wind will keep blowing
Stay grounded
Stay grounded
Let the wind blow

To Stay Whole

Before he died
I confess
My beloved was not my whole life
But he made it whole
And now
As I take this journey
I did not ask for
I am learning to be grateful for what I have
And to let go of what I don't
And this is so hard to do
To offer forgiveness
To the one who left us bereft
To offer him gratitude
While wanting more
To offer him
Our deepest love
With hearts broken wide open
From missing him
To let him go
While holding him close
To stay whole
Even, with this hole in our hearts

I Wonder

I've heard it said that
Suicide is a confession
And I wonder
What were you confessing my beloved?
That you were heartbroken?
That you were sorry to let us down?
That this life was too much for you?
That this life wasn't enough for you?
That we were not enough?
That you could not stay?
That it was "your time"?
That this life was not worth fighting for?
What could I have done
To change your mind?
Because my mind cannot make sense of this
But my answer to you my beloved
Is that you could never let us down
That our love for you has no boundaries
That joy and pain can live together
One does not exclude the other
That you were not a mistake
You were meant to be
To be here
With us
Fighting for this life
This precious life

I Don't Want This to Be My Life

I don't want this to be my life
But
It is
And so
I must find a way to make it okay
But right now
I cry every day
I feel the terrible pain of loss
I feel the shame and anger and sadness
I cannot sleep
I cannot find answers that will give me rest
I want things to be different
I want my beloved to come home
I want
I don't want this to be my life
But it is
And so
I must find a way to make it okay
Find my way back to gratitude
And some days I do
But right now
I don't want this to be my life
But it is

To Rise from the Ashes

How do you understand something that is not
    understandable?
How do you transform tragedy into triumph?
How do you find the lessons in the fire
When you are burning in the flames?
When there is no comfort
No cooling waters
Maybe it is when you surrender
Surrender into the flames
Into the pain
And then
Like the Phoenix
You rise from the ashes
Begin to put the pieces back together
Find the lesson, the gift
And learn to fly again

Let Sadness Be Your Teacher

As I search for the how of letting go
Of surrendering
Of finding my way
I have found some profound words
Words that made me stop and breathe
Made me sigh
"Let your sadness teach you" they said
"Let things that are not sad
Teach you
Let the window teach you
How to let light in . . .
Let the sadness teach you
For your sadness is the paint
You must find a canvas"*
These words give me so much hope
Hope that life will begin again
Hope that there is always new life
New ways to see the world
New ways to be in the world
Even when sadness is the teacher

*Mark Nepo in *The Book of Awakening*

If Sadness Is My Teacher

If sadness is my teacher
What am I learning?
I am learning to be quiet
To be still
To listen
To wait
To pray
I am learning to be lost
And that this is where we can be found
To be in despair
And that this is where we can find hope
To be in doubt
And that this is where we can find faith
To be in darkness
And that this is where we can find light
If sadness is my teacher
I am learning it is in surrendering
That sadness can become joy
That death can become life

No One's Fault

Today when I woke up
For the first time
I did not think of Chris as I opened my eyes
I thought of "surrender"
And then the thought came with my heart open
"It's not your fault"
My mind took that
And started the list
The list of all the reasons it was my fault
All my weaknesses, all my mistakes, all my shadows
All my humanness
And my heart kept answering
"It's not your fault"
"It's not your fault"
And then something happened
And I could take a deep breath
I could hear the words
It was not my fault
It was no one's fault
It was a perfect storm
A tragedy
A mistake
A mistake made in a moment of unconsciousness
A moment of not knowing
A moment lost in time
A moment lost forever

The Endless Sadness

Oh the sadness is deep
There is no end
To the well of grief
I can't tell
If I'm at the top looking down
Or at the bottom looking up
Either way
The sadness is endless
Yes, there are sparks of light
Sparks of life
And those
I will reach for
I will hold onto
But truth be told
The sadness is like a heavy cloak
That weighs me down that slowly softens me,
     takes me to my knees
Makes me see with different eyes
Eyes of sadness
Eyes of compassion
Eyes of the darkest wisdom

To Wait

The pain of loss comes to us all
And maybe the best we can do
Is wait
Wait until we don't need to wait anymore
Wait for time to pass
Wait for our eyes to adjust to the darkness
And then we can begin to feel our way
Feel our way to finding ourselves
Finding who we are
Now that we have this wound
This wound that has opened our heart, our mind,
    and our soul
And just as with a physical wound
It takes time
It takes care
It takes work
It takes waiting
Waiting for healing to do its work
For healing to reveal the gift
For healing to reveal the light

Not Yet a "Survivor"

Where am I?
How do I feel?
It feels like I am between worlds
Not in the world of innocence
The world before we became "survivors of suicide"
Our hearts broken wide open
And yet
Not quite in the world of survivors
Dipping my toes in it perhaps
But not emerged
Can still believe he is just away
For I can still tell myself it was an accident
And when the truth comes too close
I call back
No No No
And go on with my day
Telling myself
This is a dream
This is not my life
This could not be my life
But then I'll see the bin of basketballs
The ones he used to leave all over the driveway
The basketballs we used to play pig with
And I will come undone
For the basketballs stay in the bin now
And the pain in my heart does not go away, does not go away

A New Normal

I feel numb again
Lost in the sadness
Lost in the aching to see him again
And I know
If you are lost
There is the possibility of being found
And so
I wander through this barren land of grief
Looking for something that looks familiar
Looking for something that feels normal
And I know
That somewhere in this wilderness
There is a place to be found
There is something called a "new normal"
And oh
How I long for this new normal
Something that will look familiar
Something that will feel normal
Something that will seem like home
Like being found

There Are Many Truths

There are so many truths in this life
And sometimes
It is easier to hold on to the truth that is hurting us
Easier to see that truth
When in fact
There are many other truths
Truth that may hold us up
Truth that may be harder to find perhaps
But truth that gives us strength
For it may be true that the sky is gray and rainy
It is also true that there are blue skies and sunshine
And
It may be true that we have deep wounds within
It is also true that we are given gifts
Reasons for the heart to overflow
Reasons to keep hope alive
To keep putting one foot in front of the other
Even when we don't know where we're going
We can keep going
For the truth is
Life goes on
No matter what, truth is at your door
Life goes on

Maybe

I've tried really hard
To keep the truth away
To keep pretending it didn't happen
At least
Maybe
Not this way
To keep saying he's just away
To deny there was anything wrong
That it was a mistake
An accident
And maybe it was
That's as close as I can get right now
He is gone and it was an accident
A terrible, terrible accident
He didn't mean to take his life
And in taking his life
Maybe
He didn't mean to take a part of ours
He didn't mean to
He just didn't mean to
And maybe
He didn't know what he was doing
He didn't know he was leaving us
He didn't know he was breaking our hearts
Tearing us apart
He didn't know
He just didn't know
Maybe . . .

Melancholy

Melancholy is a good word
It kind of sounds like it feels
Sad but not despairing
Sad but with some hope
Hope for new beginnings
Hope that there is light in the darkness
That the pain will be dull
A kind of constant drumbeat
Instead of sharp, stabbing pains
That take you to your knees
At least most of the time
Melancholy
Accepting what is
In the midst of loss
In the ocean of sadness
The gentle waves of sunrise
The gentle hope of letting go
Of new beginnings

This Is Life

Someone told me
We all have light and darkness within
Light and darkness in our experience as well
One does not cancel out the other
They exist together
In our lives
In the world
In the Universe
So when something bad has happened
When we experience failure
When we are in the darkness
There is always the good as well
The successes
The light
This is life

Every Experience Lives

I understand more than ever
How pain and joy can live together
How every experience we have
Lives in our bodies, hearts, and minds
Lives in the world
In the Universe
All are true
All are one
Playing peek-a-boo with my grandson the other day
I was transported back in time
And I unknowingly said
"Where's Chris . . . where's Chris?"
Suddenly I came back to the present
And the pain of time travel
Was excruciating
The memory of playing peek-a-boo with Chris
So real
So present in my body, mind, and soul
And at the same time
In front of me
Little innocent Jacob
Smiling, laughing, playing
So present in my body, mind, and soul

Not Alone

I sat at your grave yesterday
Placed a fern there
A gift for your half birthday
I sat on the ground
And the river of tears came flooding out
I talked to you
I wondered again how could this have happened?
I told you how sorry I was
How much I missed you
How much we all miss you
And as I looked across the field
Gazing at the water fountains
At all the markers and flowers
Hundreds of them
I knew
We were not alone
You were not alone
So many others
So many others have gone before
And we all wait
For some day
When we will be together again
When we can hold you in our arms
But for now
We wait
And send you our love
Send you our hopes
Send you our dreams

Surrendering to the Darkness

We sent a lantern into the sky last night
Sent it with our love
Our hopes
Our dreams
Sent a light into the darkness
Letting it go
Surrendering it to the beyond
And we watched
As it floated farther and farther away
Higher and higher
Until at last
It had gone as far as it could go
And disappeared
Into the darkness
And as it disappeared
I could feel him leaving
Feel him letting go
Feel myself surrendering to the unknown
Surrendering to the darkness once again

How Could You Not Stay

Some days
The pain of losing you
Is so unbearable
I don't know what to do
I cry
I moan
I look for you
I beg you to come back
Knowing that you can't
The questions flood my mind
Knowing there are no answers
All I know is
I don't know . . . I don't know
I don't know
And I want to die
But no damn it
I want to live
I want to make a difference
I want to stay
I only wish
You had stayed too
How could you not stay?
How could you not stay?

How Long Will It Take

How long will it take
I wonder
To feel your presence
Even if in your absence
How long will it take
I wonder
For the ache in my heart
To feel more like gratitude
How long will it take
I wonder
For the doubt to become faith
For the despair to become hope
For the darkness to be light

Holy Ground

There was a graduation party yesterday
There were kids playing volleyball
Playing in the field where my son died
When I first heard them and saw them
My breath caught in my throat
My heart seemed to stand still
I wanted to run to the place
Beg them to stop
To leave
This holy ground
Don't you know? I wanted to scream
Don't you know?
But then a calm descended
And though I cried gently
I thought
Maybe this is a good thing
A healing thing for the earth
A healing thing for the earth
Kids playing volleyball
Laughing and playing
In the place where my son died
It is still
Holy ground
It is still
Holy ground

Time to Be One

I didn't want to admit my thought
That it's not fair
When something so bad happens
Knowing that bad things happen
They just do
And it's never fair
And maybe the best we can do
Is accept that knowing
That bad things happen
And when they do
That is the time to hold each other
Time to be together
To stay connected
To be one
To be love

Hold On

I've been driving myself crazy lately
Imagining all the ways I could have saved him
Asking myself why didn't I
I should have know
I'm his mother
I should have felt something
Called him
Told him to wait a minute
I'd call his brother
I'd call his sister
Get him help
And call him right back
I'd tell him to hold on
Help is on the way
Please, please
Hold on
Help is on the way
I'd get there too
As quickly as I could
Be there tomorrow
Come from the airport
Straight to the hospital
We'd be there
Holding his hands
We'd cry together
We'd work it out
Just
Please, please
Hold on
Please, please
Hold on

Growing toward the Light

Nature teaches us
To grow
We have to grow toward the light
Always go toward the light
To heal
To come out of the darkness
We have to be gentle
We have to be strong
We have to open and surrender
Just as the flower
Breaking through the earth
We have to go toward the light
Live life with gratitude
Live a life of simplicity
And compassion
Growing toward the light

One Teardrop at a Time

I can hardly breathe sometimes
Knowing you are gone
But life goes on
And so must we
So we pick up the pieces of our lives
The pieces we can carry on with
And just carry on
Doing the best we can
Remembering how to love
Doing what we can to honor you
Missing you still
Wishing with all our hearts we could change what happened
Knowing that we can't
And so what choice do we have
But to remember you
And carry on, though the tears still flow
Be strong, be steadfast
Walk the path of healing
One day at a time
One step at a time
One teardrop at a time

It Is Not Possible

One year ago today was your last day
And I keep wondering
Did you know it was your last?
I can't imagine that
That is impossible
It was a beautiful day
Your friends were all around you
Swimming, laughing, talking
You went golfing
You got your hair cut
You made plans for the future
You ordered a watch
You could not have thought it was your last day
You took pictures
You posted pictures and words
Oh your words
"friends . . . good times . . . going away party . . . love . . .
      happy . . . niece . . . happy"
You could not have thought it was to be your last day
At your own hand
It is not possible
It is not possible

To Let It Be

One year without you
One year missing you
One year remembering you
One year being grateful
Grateful
For all you were
And all you continue to be
A light in darkness
Guiding our steps
Sending us signs
Being so ever present
Never far from our thoughts
Always in our hearts
Giving us strength
Teaching us to be
Teaching us to let it be

My Wish

I wish I could have held him
That's all
I wish I could have held him

The First Step

I think it happened yesterday
I hit rock bottom
As I lay curled up on the floor
Crying, crying, crying
In my mind begging him to come home
Thinking about all the things I could have done
What I could have done differently
How I could have made everything right
It was then that a gentle voice beside me said
This is the first step
When you see you are powerless
I got so angry then
Angry that there was nothing I could do
So angry, that something broke inside of me
I laid on the ground
Feeling so helpless, so weak, so defeated
All resistance gone
And that is what it took
To find a strength within
Strength to carry on
To feel some peace
To see some light
To find the courage to try again
To begin again
To let go of the fear, the shame, the anger
To let it be, to ask for help

Breaking Open

Today
Is a day I hoped would never come
Had convinced myself would never come
The day we give my son back to Mother Earth
The silent earth
The earth that gives us life
But today
She takes him back into her womb
And I
I am scared, scared I will break
Left with an ache in my heart
The reality sinking in
He will never come home
The reality that will break me
Break me wide open
And I can only hope
That this breaking open
Is in the way the flower breaks open
The butterfly
The heart
For when we break like that
There is hope
Hope that there will be beauty
Will be flight
Will be life

The Sunflower

Today is the day I've been dreading
Been trying to run away from
But the faster I ran
The closer I came
And just as I thought I couldn't go on
I looked around my garden and there growing out of the
    gravel
And next to the grill
Where he always did his grilling
Bloomed a bright yellow sunflower
One I did not plant
One that was not blooming yesterday
It just appeared
With a personality as big as Christopher
Standing there
Smiling it seemed
And telling me I could go on
Telling me even in the brokenness
The sun will keep shining
I will see him again
All is well
Let it be

Who Held You Last?

Who held you last
Our sweet, sweet Chris?
Mother Earth held you
With infinite tenderness
I imagine you sometimes
Lying in the field
The trees watching over you
Protecting you
The sky, the moon, the stars
Until morning came
And the sun brought those who could help
The trees still watching
Witnessing your struggle
And then your resting
Who will hold you for all time
Our sweet, sweet Chris?
Mother Earth will hold you
With infinite tenderness
Mother Earth
Who gives us life
Mother Earth
Whose heart is filled with love
She will cradle you
In the sands of time
Embracing you with care
Whispering to you, the wind her breath
The blue sky, her mind
The green leaves pulsing with her blood
The rain her water of life

And you, you will become all of this
As she is holding you
Mother Earth
With infinite tenderness
Sweet peace be yours, our sweet, sweet Chris
"Deep peace of the quiet earth be yours"

Closer and Further Away

What happens on the day after
The day after you return the ashes of your beloved
To the womb of the Earth
There is some comfort
Believing he can go now
Believing we have let go
There is some comfort
The day has come and gone
Knowing we are perhaps another day closer
Closer to seeing him again
But it is another day further away from him
Further away from his hugs and smiles
From his humor and sarcasm
From his care and compassion
Further away from him
From memories of him
This is new territory
To be closer
And yet
To be further away

My Heart Is Holding You

My heart is holding you
My broken heart is holding you
Will always be holding you
Though my arms ache for you
To hold you close
To feel the warmth of you next to me
My eyes long to see you
To see the love in your eyes
To see your smile
My ears long to hear your voice
The kindness and the truth you spoke
Your reassuring words
My hands long to touch you
To feel your cheeks in my hands
To stroke your hair
But my heart
My broken heart
Is holding you
Will always be holding you

You Had to Leave

Someone said to me
Sometimes
Some people just have to leave
I wish with all my heart and soul
That you were not one of them
One who just had to leave
Leaving us confused and hurting
But always loving you
Always remembering you
Keeping you with us
In whatever ways we can
Even though
You had to leave
You had to leave

Love Stays

I cannot change what has happened
Though it breaks my heart
To think you are gone
But somehow, you are always with me
And all I can do
Is be with this
Accept this
Remember you
Always remember you
And I will stay
Because that's what love does
Love stays
Love stays and accepts what is
Love stays and grows and changes
Love stays
Love stays

There Is Love

Sometimes
When the waves of grief overtake me
There is a peace that flows as well
A peace that lets the tears fall like raindrops
A peace that "passes all understanding"
And maybe it is because the tears are truth
Because the sadness and pain are allowed
And when they are allowed
There is acceptance of what is
And in the acceptance is love

I Can Go On

Every morning
When I go out to swim
There are little frogs and insects in the pool
Hanging on for dear life
And one by one
I reach for them
And as tenderly as I can
Scoop them out of the water
And return them to the earth
Where they scamper off
Given another chance
To take a quiet breath
And I sigh
My heart filling with gratitude and compassion
And the knowing
That if I can still love
I can go on

Missing Someone

There are times
When missing someone
Fills us with confusion
Turmoil and pain
But then
There are other times
When missing someone
Brings us such clarity
Such clear understanding
About what matters
About what doesn't matter too
About what we can change
And what we cannot change
And it brings us close to the truth
The truth that life is all about love
Love for all
Love for what is
Love for what isn't
Love for what might have been
Love for what may be
Love for life

Not All of Me

There is a wisdom teaching
That says
When we have been hurt
Deeply hurt
There is a part of us
That is unharmed
There is a part of us
That can see there is light
Even in the darkest darkness
Can know there is clarity
In the confusion
Can feel the hope
Within the despair
So even though there is great sadness
I know
It is a part of me
It is not all of me

Since He Left

Since he left
Our beautiful boy
Since he left
I've asked myself a million times
How did this happen
Asked myself what did I miss
And the answer always comes back to me
It wasn't your fault
It wasn't anyone's fault
It was an accident
It was a mistake
That shouldn't have happened
But it did
And it couldn't be fixed
And so we are left
Lost in the darkness with so many others
But we are learning to live our lives with more care perhaps
Being more present
Allowing the darkness to teach us
Allowing the light to hold us

It Is Said

It is said
That only time
Can put the past in perspective
Only time can lay the past to rest
So that
Your future can be new
Your future can lie before you
Held up perhaps
By the lessons of the past
Opened perhaps
By the broken heart
By surrender to what is
So that
In time
The past is in perspective
The present and the future
A blank page
An open book
Held with care
Held with hope
Hope for the unfolding mystery
That is life
Hope for love and light and peace
That is grace
That is past, present, and future

There When I Need It

Sometimes
Something in our life feels like an obligation
And that's how it felt at first
Going to the cemetery
Making sure his grave was tidy
Making sure the grass didn't go over the marker
Watering the plant, changing the flowers
But then I started to pause
Though I was afraid to be still
When I was still
I felt a tug to kneel
To be close to the earth
Knowing he wasn't really there
But feeling his presence anyway
And now
It feels like this obligation has changed
Now it is something that is there
When I need it
A place to go
A place of peace and quietness
A place to be still

I Just Wonder

I wonder sometimes
How mystery might be a part of my life
What things may come to me
That may be signs
Signs of someone who listens
Someone who hears our crying, our hopes
Someone who sees our tears and our broken hearts
I wonder sometimes
What angels have passed me on the path
Bringing me consolation
Giving me courage
The sweet words of truth
The gentle touch on my shoulder
The soft breeze on my cheek
The loving glance
I wonder sometimes
I just wonder

Stay Standing

I've been learning to fall down
And to get up again
It seems to be the story of my life
Or maybe it is my life lesson
When you fall down
You get up
When you feel the sting of rejection
You surrender
Surrender and get up
Get up and move forward
Keep learning the lesson
When you fall down
Though the pain is enough to level you
Get up
Until one day
You can stay standing
Even if it is just inside yourself
You are standing
You are strong
You know you are enough
Enough
Just as you are

An Ending, A Beginning

It is curious to me
That today
A few days after I no longer knew
Which way to go
A sense of peace envelops me
Like a soft and warm blanket
I am filled with acceptance
Acceptance of who I am
A dark and heavy cloak
Has been lifted from my shoulders
I feel courage and strength and freedom
I feel myself surrendering once again
Knowing this is an ending
Knowing this is a beginning

Home with Ourselves

Life has many lessons
And one we must learn
Along the way
Tells us that happiness is an inside job
I am not responsible for another's happiness
And no one else is responsible for mine
And to be happy
We have only to open our hearts
Surrender to what is
Live where we are
Open that door
Walk in and find ourselves at home
No need to be lost
No need to hide
To be happy
All we need
Is to be at home
Home with ourselves

To Open My Heart

To open my heart
I'm finding
I have to open my hands
And open my arms
To let others in
I have to offer my heart
Give what I have to give
Do what I am able to do
Go where they need me to go
While I stay with myself
While I am myself
Doing what I need to do
Taking care of myself
While I offer that care to others
To open my heart
I have to open my hands
Have to open my arms

Opening to Life

Sitting on a rock the other day
One in the woods
One covered with moss
I was just listening to the sounds of nature
The birds chattering
The wind whistling through the trees
The squirrel scampering by
And every once in a while
The ping, ping, ping of a falling acorn
The ending of one cycle of life
The beginning of another
As it landed in the arms of Mother Earth
To be held and nurtured
Until it too would open to the life within
The roots, the trunk, the branches and leaves
Opening to the rain and the sky
Growing toward the light
Opening to the light
Opening to life

Fourteen Months

Nature seems to match my mood today
This day that marks fourteen months
Fourteen months since you left
It doesn't sound like very long
And when I glanced at your picture
The tears began to flow
A bit unexpectedly
But there they were
And I surrendered to them
As I cried
It rained outside
As I moaned
The wind blew
As I rocked back and forth
The tree's branches blew back and forth too
And as I allowed this wave of grief
The clouds opened for a moment
Revealing blue skies behind the grayness
Sunshine behind the darkness

Again

I have come back around
To asking questions that have no answers
How did this happen
It can't be true
My heart breaks all over again
And I just don't understand
How this could be
And so
I have to go back to finding my way
To surrendering to the only answer there is
And that is
There is no answer
It will never make sense
It will never be okay
It will be
Just as the seasons
Something I come back to
Again and again and again

With What Is

Someone asked
How do we survive our own lives?
And the answer came back
We all ask this all the time
And what a relief I felt
You mean we don't have to have it all figured out?
You mean we don't have to have all the answers?
You mean we don't always have to know what is best?
You mean we live our lives one day at a time?
We can be with what is
See where it takes us
And know
That
Sometimes
We just need to surrender . . .
Surrender, surrender, surrender

Let the Wisdom In

I don't know why it is
That you can hear something many times
And yet, not hear it
It doesn't sink in
Until one day
It just does
And it's like a light being turned on
And you get it
As I got it this morning
The words I read
Sinking slowly through my mind, my body, and my spirit
Words that said don't worry about what to do, or how
But just let the wisdom in
The wisdom to survive
The wisdom to grow and change

Hiding in Plain Sight

Sometimes
Things happen
Things we see coming
And yet don't see
Like a train coming toward us
But we fail to move
Fail to see what is in front of us
Until it's too late
And then
There we are
Trying to sort things out
Trying to find the lesson
In the pain
When the lesson
Was there all along
Hiding in plain sight
Waiting for us to open our eyes
Waiting for us to see

Balance

Life
It seems
Is about figuring it out
Every day
Figuring out the balance
The balance to be, to heal, to love
It is the balance
To be in relationship
To work things out
So there is peace
So there is serenity
So there is balance

To Keep Going

There's an expression that runners use
They say they "hit the wall"
When the body is so tired
When the heart and spirit are empty
And they think they can't go on
And what they must learn in order to win
Is to keep going
Even when they hit the wall
And it is the same in life
Sometimes
We all hit the wall in different ways
Feel like we can't go on
The lessons are too hard
The pain too sharp
The wound too deep
But the human spirit is resilient
We can go on
Even when our hearts are breaking
The secret to life
Sometimes
It seems
Is to keep going
Even when you hit the wall

My Truth

I am learning
That my truth
Is just that
It is my truth
And though it may not be truth for someone else
I must follow what is mine to follow
I must not allow other voices
Or the voice of my own ego
To lead me down another's path
For my path has value
My path needs to be traveled
And as I learn my truths
The way will be clear
The way of my heart
The way of inner wisdom

Love

There is a teaching
That says when we judge another
It is because we have done the same
But we have denied it
And when we take the blinders off our eyes
And off our hearts
We can see the truth
We will let the fear go
And there will be the answer
And the answer is love
Love instead of fear
Love instead of judgment
Love is always the answer
The answer to all that troubles us
To all that disconnects us
To all that separates us

To Choose Life

Sometimes
We think we have no choices
But today
I choose to believe
To believe that we do have choices
Choices to live as if it matters
This life matters
With all its heartache and darkness
With all its joy and light
It matters enough
To care about walking gently on the earth
To love with kindness and compassion
To speak the truth
It matters enough
To choose life
With all its ups and downs
With all its peace and turmoil
This is the life we have
So why not choose it
Choose life
Choose love
Choose gratitude

Waiting for Him

I thought I saw him the other day
I started to say his name
Call to him
But just as quickly
I realized it couldn't be him
That a part of me knows he is gone
Gone forever
But a part of me still hopes
Hopes there's been a mistake
That he didn't really leave
Not like that
Not forever
And I guess I'll always hope
And always wait
Wait for him to come home

Trusting Myself

I've been learning about unconditional love
And learning how to love myself
And so
I'm beginning again
At the beginning
Looking at photos of my younger self
Asking her where she is
Asking her to come home
Telling her she is safe
And I imagine her
Peeking out from behind closed doors
Looking out to see if it is true
That I will trust her
That I will be with her
Love her
Become one with her

A New Ending

It's Veterans Day today
And I listened to the story of two friends
Caught in gunfire on the battlefield
One was hit and went down
Calling out to his comrades
"Help, I need help"
And there began his journey to recovery
Being humbled by his weakness
But being strengthened by his will to keep going
To keep fighting for a new life
And today
That is what I find myself doing
Fighting for a new life
Not because I've been hit by gunfire
But because I need a new ending to my story
And so
I have to say "Help, I need help"
And then I need to keep going
Keep fighting for a new life
For a new ending to my story

Destiny

It is said that some of life is destiny
That there is a secret destination
One that we cannot know
And as we go about our days and nights
We move toward that secret place
That place where your truth waits for you
That place where the lessons of your life lead you
And that place where you will find peace
Where you will find home
And for some the road is hard
The road is long
And yet
There is light in the darkness
Warmth in the cold
Hope in the despair

We Can Make It

The wise ones,
They say
Pain has its purposes
Pain has its lessons
And those lessons teach us
Teach us to keep going
To go through our transitions
To lean into our pain
To build bridges to the other side
To open to love
To wisdom
To the knowing that everything will be okay
We just have to believe
That no matter what
We can make it
No matter what
We can make it

All Will Be Well

It seems to me
That the secret way to peace
Is to be open to what is
We don't know what is best for us
So if we could see what is in front of us
What is around us
And be okay with it
Even if it means changing it
First be open to it
Let all the feelings in
The love, the hate, the resistance, the joy
The grief, the pain, the anger, the love
Let it all in
Open to it all
All will be well

What Good Could There Be

They say there is grace that comes from suffering
But my God
How could you take my son?
How?
Why would you take my son?
What grace could there possibly be
What grace was in his suffering
Suffering that took his life
God damn it
I want to know
Why did this happen
What good could there possibly be
I beg of you
Anyone
I beg of you
Tell me what good might come
Tell me
What good

Grace

There is so much pain in the world
So much suffering
And the work we do to heal
Is the deepest work of all
It asks so much of us
To be vulnerable
To ask for help
To surrender
To fall to our knees
And when we fall to our knees
Then there is hope
Hope that you will find the strength you need
Hope that you will know your truth
And when you know your truth
You will be free
You will be full of grace

Breathe in Love

The yoga teacher was leading us through a meditation
Breathe in love she said
All that is good, all that is positive is love
Breathe it in
Breathe out fear she said
All that is negative is fear
Breathe it out
And that was a surprise to me
At the bottom of everything
There is love
Or
There is fear
I can see that now
And so, yes
Breathe in love
Breathe out fear
Love allows us to heal, to change, to grow
Fear makes us weak, anxious, and small
Breathe in love
Breathe out fear

The Key

I dreamed I was in a jail
And the jailors were different parts of me
My fear, my judge, my doubt, my despair
And I dreamed I had the key to the lock
And I could open the lock
Open the door to the jail of my own making
And beyond the jail
Lay open fields
And an expanse of sky
And as I left the jail
The jail of my own making
The message was clear
You cannot get lost
On this journey
Your journey
You may wander around a bit
But you cannot get lost
For you hold within
The wisdom you need
The key to your freedom
The key to your life

For Now

My heart is so heavy
I hardly know what to do
The memories flooding back
The words spoken
The words left unsaid
I try to talk to him
Silence comes back to me
I ask for guidance
Sadness comes back to me
And so
I think
That is where I need to be
In the silence
In the sadness
At least for now
At least, for now

Being You

It is so hard to move out of the sadness
To let go of the suffering
For in letting go
You are asked to let go of the one who could not live
You have to find a way to live
Holding him in your heart
But moving forward without him
It feels like too much sometimes
But somehow
If you keep choosing life
Keep choosing hope
Keep choosing faith and happiness
Then one day
You will become these things
Become life and hope, faith and happiness
And still
He will be there
A part of you
Always a part of you
Melting into you
Being you

To Life

My life has fallen apart it seems
My son
My beloved son has slipped away
My husband has gone his separate way
Rejecting "us" he said
Not me or him but us
And so my life may look like I have failed
But that is not what I see
I see a life that matters
A life of giving and receiving
Of love and gratitude
A life full with children and grandchildren
My heart aching for what has been lost
But alive with what has been found
Love and hope and light
Gentle breezes
Blue skies
Red roses
And most of all
Breathing in love
Breathing out fear
Allowing life to take me
Surrendering to what is
To life
Always to life

A Story to Live

There is a song I learned
"Doors opening
Doors closing
I am safe
It's only change"
And as I keep walking this path
Opening doors
Closing doors
Opening doors
It seems clear to me
That we always get to choose
And sometimes
The best thing to do
Is to close a door
Let that story go
For there is always another door
A door to open
A story to live
A story to tell

New Year's Day

It's New Year's Day today
A day to look back
A day to look forward
The sorrows of yesterday still heavy on my heart
The tears still fall
Nearly every day
But there are days
When I feel the warmth of the sun
Notice the way Mother Earth goes through this season
This season of darkness
Quietly, the trees bare and still
The ground cold and hard
And I think
This is my wintertime too
Time to be quiet
Time to still my mind
Time to heal my heart
And wait
Wait for the spring breezes
And signs of new life
Wait for life to feel safe again

Lost

I wonder when the feeling of emptiness leaves
Knowing he will never come back
Knowing he left on purpose
It doesn't matter that he didn't know what he was doing
It doesn't matter that people say he is at peace
He is still gone
And the pain is so deep
I can't bring myself to believe it happened
Not this way
Dear God
Not this way
What did I miss
I have to believe
There was nothing we missed
To live, to survive, to stay sane
I have to believe
There was nothing we missed
It was, as they say, a perfect storm
It came out of nowhere
And in an instant
It was over
Just like a tornado, or hurricane or blizzard
It was over
And he was lost
Lost to that perfect storm

Home

Sometimes the way home
Is long and hard and silent
You just have to keep getting up in the morning
Keep putting one foot in front of the other
Keep watching, keep listening
Keep waiting, keep seeking
Until one day
It begins to feel like you belong again
Belong to life
Belong at home
Home with yourself
Home with all that is
Home with all that is not

Broken and Yet Whole

We've all got missing pieces
We all have broken hearts
And maybe that's where we can find ourselves
Can find each other
In the brokenness
In the emptiness
Somehow
We can bring the pieces together
Mend the broken hearts
And find wholeness
In being together
For we are all one
Unique and yet the same
Broken and yet whole

You Are Not Here

There will never be closure
For the hole in my heart
It will forever be
The aching inside of me
Even as I heal
The aching does not go away
It is with me morning, noon, and night
A constant reminder
That you are not here
With every breath
With every sigh
With every tear
You are not here
And my heart breaks a little bit more
With every smile
With every laugh
With every song
Because you are not here
Because there will never be a way back
A way back to you

To Tend to the Brokenness

I have been learning
In the weeks and months since you left
That sometimes
Words have sharp edges
Very sharp edges
When your heart has been broken
Words can deepen the wound
Just as surely as a knife
And though they are tossed about
In thoughtless ways
In unknowing ways
They leave the tender heart to bleed
And so
Sometimes
Silence is the only answer
Silence is the only way
Because there are no words
That are soft enough
To tend the brokenness within

You Get to Choose

There are times when nothing makes sense
When your world has turned upside down
When your child has died
And your partner has left
How are you to make sense of anything again?
No matter how many times
You go over things in your mind
The things you said
The things you didn't say
The things you did
The things you didn't do
The things you saw
The things you didn't see
There is no way to make sense of it
For you become undone
And there's nothing you can do to change what has been
But you can choose
Every day you wake up
You get to choose
How to put the pieces back together
How to be in the world now that so much is lost
And as for me
I choose life
I choose peace
I choose hope
I choose being found

Life Is Beautiful

Every time I say I'm doing good
Every time I smile and say I'm fine
Something inside of me breaks
Because my heart knows
It's not the truth
It could never be the truth
Not now
Not ever
But I break through the pain
And say I'm all right
Because my heart knows
My heart knows the truth
And my heart doesn't let go
But my heart chooses life
Chooses hope
Chooses love
And my heart knows
Life is beautiful
Even with the pain
Even with the truth
Life is beautiful

There Is Peace

When I think about all the pain in the world
It is good to remember
The yoga teaching
To breathe in love
To breathe out fear
And to know
That everything is about love
It is either giving love
Or it is a call for love
And so
It seems we are called to love
We are called to give unconditional grace
And with love
With grace
There is forgiveness
There is peace

The Deepest Pain

They say even the deepest pain will pass
Although it doesn't feel like it
If we can see the bigger picture
Feel our pain from that perspective
If we can believe there is a bigger reality
Perhaps even a reason for this pain
Then maybe
Just maybe
We can heal
And the deepest pain will pass

Enough

Someone said life is the journey
The road is home
We are what we are looking for
We are who we seek
And so
It seems
If we could stop our wandering
Be with what is
Be with who we are
That would be enough
That would always be enough

The Question

It is said by those who are wise
You already have what you're looking for
The answers are inside
But sometimes
The hardest thing to know
The most difficult thing to find
Is what is the question?
For if we knew the question
Perhaps all our seeking
All our yearning and longing
Would know where to look
To find the answer
To see the truth
To know what it is
We're looking for

Letting Go

Letting go seems so hard to do
Especially when the letting go
Is of one who is such a part of me
My love so deep
My longing so complete
And yet
In the letting go
I can still hold on
Hold on to the parts of you
That just have to stay
You have to stay in the morning
When I greet you with the sun, and send you a blessing
You have to stay during the day
When I tell you what's going on with us
And how we wish you were here
You have to stay in the evening
When I tell you how much I love you
How much I miss you
You have to stay in the night
When I tell you good night
Tell you how I would change everything if I could
Have you back here with us if only we could
And then I tell you thank you
Thank you for being a part of my life
Thank you for staying
Even though I let you go, even though I must let go

Love Is the Key

I hope that some day
I will truly believe
All is as it must be
We each have our path to walk
And for some
The journey is hard
For some
It is far too short
But no matter the story
There is a bigger story
And we each play our part
And all we need to know
Is love is the key
That unlocks the door
Unlocks the door to love
To peace
To joy

Without Saying Good-Bye

Sometimes
There is a sadness so deep
There is no way out
Just like floating in the ocean
I float on this sea of sadness
Not always able to see the beginning nor the end
So many days blend together
Days I was perhaps fully present
But more days when I came and went
Saw a glimpse in his eye
Felt the hesitation of his smile
And yet, did not see it for what it was
For he too was floating in the ocean
Unable to see the beginning nor the end
And in that deep sadness
Was saying good-bye
Was leaving us
Without saying good-bye
Leaving us
Without saying good-bye

Go Where Life Would Love You

I guess we all reach crossroads
Places where we choose
Choose the journey ahead
While letting the old journey fade away
Because its foundation became too unsettled
Shifted too far one way or the other
And so a new journey begins
And if you can stay awake
The direction of the new journey
Comes from within
And when this is the case
You get to follow your heart
Set your own course
Set your own sails
Face the storms
Rest into the sun
Float with the gentle breezes
And not be afraid
Choose love
Choose peace
Let go of fear
Spread your wings
And go
Go where life would have you
Where life would love you
Just you, just the way you are

New Beginning

I am waiting
Waiting for a new beginning to my life
Even as all I see are endings
I open
I surrender
I grieve
I wait
Wait for the winter in me to end
Wait for my heart to stop breaking
For warmth to fill my soul
For my soul to be free once more
For spring to come again
The earth beneath my feet
To be steady once more
To be solid
To be offering new beginnings
To be full of life once more

Moments and Memories

There is a Dr. Seuss quote
That says
"Sometimes you will never know
The value of a moment
Until it becomes a memory"
And I know the truth of that
In all the memories
That stay close to my heart
Memories of moments in time
The extra hug
The glance that held unspoken words
The look over his shoulder that told me he loved life
The look on his face as he stood by the lake, arms
    stretched out
And smiling that unmistakable smile
Just moments in time
But oh! The memories they have made
The memories that remind me life has changed
But life is good
The memories that heal my broken heart

The Light of Truth

I feel like I've been floundering in the dark
That those voices in my head
The ones that tell me I'm not good enough
Have been running my life
And I—I have been living a lie
For those voices are just tricksters
Blaming me
And shaming me
For things that are not mine to carry
For things that are too heavy to carry alone
And now
Now I see how confused I have been
How I have followed the wrong voices
The ones that lead me
Around and around
Back to the darkness
Always back to the darkness
And it is with a heavy heart
That I see a light
Off in the distance
A light leading to the bridge
The bridge of understanding
The bridge that will lead me out of the darkness
Into the light of life
Into the light of truth

All We Need

Here I stand
In the heartache
And in the truth
For even the deepest pain
Has a truth to touch us
A lesson to learn
And maybe the lesson
In the pain
Tells us
Life goes on
Life always goes on
And there is beauty in the pain
There is even life in the pain
For now I know
The only truth is love
Love is all we need
To give
To receive
To see
All we need
Is love

We Keep Going

It's hard to explain
How we keep going
When life has been so cruel
When life has dealt us such a searing pain
But go on we do
One day at a time
One moment at a time
Carrying what has hurt us
Falling apart sometimes
And standing back up
Putting the pieces of our lives back together
In a new way
In a way that grows hope
That holds the light for our hearts
And then holds the light for others
Those who come behind us
Their hearts broken
Just as ours have been
And now, though we never forget
We let go
We heal
We keep going

On Doing Wonderfully

Someone told me I was doing "wonderfully" yesterday
And somehow
That washed my foundation away
All my strength and courage collapsed
And the tidal wave of tears flowed again
For I should not be doing "wonderfully"
My life has fallen apart
The thoughts that I should have done more have returned
I should have known
I should have been able to change what happened
Why can't I change what happened
It was a terrible mistake
Why can't I go back
Start all over again
Make it right
Oh my God
Why?

When You Fall Apart

A strange thing happens when you let yourself fall apart . . .
You can begin to put yourself together again
Piece by piece
Day by day
You begin to see clearly again
You begin to see what works
What doesn't
You begin to feel whole again
You begin to see
That you are doing the best you can
Just like everyone else
You're doing the best you can
Until you fall apart again . . .

I Choose Love

Sometimes it's really hard to stay positive
There is so much sadness and fear
So much struggle in the world
So much suffering
But then I remind myself
There is so much to appreciate
So much goodness and love
So much beauty in the world
The blue sky
The bright sun
Green grass and flowers of every color
Trees and leaves
Raindrops and cool breezes
People helping people
Yes
So much to appreciate
So much to love
And that is what I choose
I choose love

You Never Know

To live
No matter what
That is what I want to do
But not just live
I want to live with a grateful heart
Grateful for each day
Each hour
Each moment
Because life is worth every breath
And you never know
When your last breath will come
And when your last breath will go

Death as My Teacher

It is a great paradox
That of all the teachers in life
Death is the greatest teacher
It teaches all of us that our days are numbered
We must find a balance
Between taking care of ourselves
And taking care of others
Between being who we are
And being where we are
Between staying
And going
Holding on
And letting go

A Cycle to Everything

There is a teaching
That comes from nature
That tells us
There is a cycle to everything
And one of the cycles
Is winter and spring
Darkness and light
Rest and growth
And so I rest
Rest in the knowing
That spring will come
Light will come
Growth will come

To Rest

I hit one of those emotional walls last night
I told Chris good night
Like I do every night
Glancing at his picture
And then I cried
And cried until I fell asleep
Ah . . . sweet sleep
It feels so good to fall into your arms
Into the void
Where there is relief from the pain
A chance to get away
To rest
To hope
To find the strength once more
To move a little bit more
In the direction of healing
In the direction of letting go

He Is With Us

It's curious how some things happen
The Universe nudges you
And you call
Just when I needed that call
That reminder that I'm not alone
And sometimes I think that nudge comes from him
I think I feel him with me
Just when I miss him the most
I'll feel him looking over my shoulder
Saying I'm still with you
I'll look at his picture
And see a certain look in his eyes
That says
I see you
And I know
Somehow I know
He is with me
He is with us
Staying close by
Even as he is so far away

There Is Rest

The waves of grief
Keep coming
But just as the waves of the ocean
They recede as well
Giving us rest
From the pain
From the ache inside
That never really goes away
But it fades
From time to time
Just as the waters
Disappear into the sand
Just as the sun sets
There is rest
Though it may be dark
Maybe because it is dark
There is rest

One Step at a Time

This grief is a lot like life
You have to walk the path at your own pace
Slow down when you need to
Rest when the darkness overtakes you
Reach for the light
When it's there for you
Grow if you can
Change when you need to
Be with what is
And keep walking
One day at a time
One step at a time

There Is Still Light

It is said
That we are not our pain
And that is hard to remember
Especially on some days
When the pain is so searing
When you have trouble remembering
Remembering what it's like
To be without pain
When you have trouble remembering
That there is still love when you're lonely
There is still hope when you're despairing
There is still faith when you're doubting
There is still light when you're in the darkness

Something New

Someone told me
We don't have to start over
Just start something new
Something new . . .
And I wonder what might that be?
Maybe believing there is a reason
A reason for life as it is
With its difficulties and its suffering
Something new
Maybe believing in the Universe
To sort things out
And make meaning of the impossible
Maybe believing
Just believing
That life goes on
And there is beauty in that
And there is beauty
In just that
In just believing

Strong Enough

Sometimes I wonder
If I'll ever feel light and free again
The heaviness of my heart
Is so deep
So dark
But then there are days
When the light shines through
My heart feels open
And life seems worth the struggle
But there are those days
When I'd rather keep my eyes closed
Keep the world out
Stay with the darkness
Until I can let the light in
Ever so slowly
So I can see again
See that life is beautiful
Life is good
And I am strong enough
To see through the darkness

A Deep Breath Away

Sometimes
I find I am just a deep breath away
A moment of silence away
From the pain of losing you
Just a heartbeat away
From falling apart again
But sometimes
I find I'm just a deep breath away
From feeling you next to me
A heartbeat away
From feeling your arm on my shoulder
And sometimes
Just the flutter of my eyelids closing
And there you are
The warmth of your smile
Flowing over me
The tenderness of your eyes
Just a glance away
And there you are
Reminding me
You are not so far away
You are just a deep breath away

Everything Changes

It's amazing
How quickly everything changes
Everything seems to be moving
Moving toward healing
And then it's like a bolt of lightning strikes
And everything seems to fall apart
I'll be feeling hopeful for a day or two
And then I'm on the ground again
Crying and crying
Until I can't cry anymore
And everything has changed again
Back to hoping
Back to thinking it will be okay
But then
There is that feeling in my stomach again
The heaviness begins to weigh on my heart again
And I know what is coming
I know I'll be down on the ground again
Begging you to come home
Begging the Universe to change this story
Begging the Universe to send me help
To please, please send me help
But no one knows
And that's okay
Because I'm back to moving forward again
Back to moving toward healing

You Have to Choose

There comes a day
Or maybe it has to come every day
For an ocean of days
That you choose life
And not just life
But you have to choose happiness
Hope, faith, love
You have to choose peace
You have to decide
And keep deciding
That life is worth the struggle
And that
Just as all of life reaches for the light
We, too, have to reach
Have to open
Have to choose love
Have to choose to stay
To stay
And to grow

Surrender

Every time I go to the cemetery
And I kneel at your grave
The earth pulling me
Holding me
I read the words carefully, slowly
"Angels walk among us
Christopher James Lanier
December 25, 1988
August 4, 2013"
A part of me can never believe it
A part of me keeps saying no
This cannot be true
But I go to the cemetery
I bring you roses
I kneel at your marker
The earth still pulling me
Still holding me
And I release the roses, one petal at a time
Letting them go with the wind
And I whisper
"I surrender" as each petal floats away
Even as part of me says no
I surrender
Until one day, maybe
There will only be
Surrender

Just for a Moment

I saw you the other day
Just for a moment
But oh—my heart cracked open
To see you again
You were walking along beside some friends
Out for a walk with their dogs
You were talking and smiling
And then you paused
Looked up at me and smiled
Just for a moment
And then you were gone
Just as quickly as you had come
And my heart
My heart sang
And for the first time
In a long time
I thought
My God, my God
Walk with me
I am broken
Come walk with me

What Do You Say

What do you say?
When a six-year-old asks
What happened to her "uncle brudder"?
The one who loved her so much
The one who drew pictures with her
Played on the keyboard with her
Played on the floor with her
What do you say?
When a six-year-old asks
With her eyes so innocent
What happened to her "uncle brudder"?
The one who was always looking into those eyes
The one who watched the fireworks with her
Played in the sand with her
What can you say?
He made a mistake
It wasn't your fault
He loved you to the moon and back
But he made a mistake
A huge mistake
And he can't come back
But he still loves you
Loves you to the moon
But he can't come back

Shipwreck

It's hard
Not to feel like a shipwreck sometimes
To lay at the bottom of the ocean
In the darkness
In the stillness
In the quiet but then maybe
If you're not down too deep
A ray of light will find its way to you
And you'll move toward the light
Come up for air
And the breath
It feels so good
Though it burns at first
And the light hurts your eyes
But then maybe
You feel the breeze on your skin
And just as in the song "Sailboat"
You hope and you pray
That this wind blows you home
That you'll make it
Make it back home

With Eyes Closed

Sometimes
I close my eyes
And I don't want to open them
It feels so safe
In the darkness
It feels like I can get away
Stay away from what hurts me
So that
If I keep my eyes closed
And just breathe
The truth won't find me
But the truth grows in the darkness
In the quiet
In the stillness
Until all I can do
Is open my eyes
See what is possible to see
And then
Go back to the darkness
Go back to the quiet
And the stillness
Just as a flower in the springtime
Reaches for the light
Opens and is touched by the light
Just to go back to the quiet earth
Back to the darkness
Until it is time
To reach for the light once more
To open
To surrender

Live through These Hands

I remember holding his face in my hands
Memorizing every part of him
Knowing this would be the last time
I knew I would never see him again
Never touch him again
And so
I held him in my hands
And I understood in that moment
I would live through these hands
For the rest of my life
Holding things with care
Touching those I love
With tenderness
Touching those I meet
With gentleness
Being with them through these hands
These hands that held his face
These hands that reach for my heart
This heart that knows
There is a time to hold on
There is a time to let go

How Many Tears

How much can the human spirit withstand?
How many tears does it take to heal?
An ocean of tears
Sometimes it takes an ocean of tears
But just as winter becomes spring
Becomes summer, becomes fall
Becomes winter again
Everything in life is a process
Always a process
Sometimes
Being born feels like dying
Sometimes
Dying feels like being born
But spring
Spring will always come

To Forgive Yourself

Sometimes
The hardest thing to do
Is to forgive yourself
For what you didn't know
Forgive yourself
And know
There was nothing you could have done
Nothing you could have changed
That a destiny finds itself
Somehow
A destiny finds itself
And you may be despairing
But not without hope
You may be lost
But not without direction

My Heart Heals

I heard his voice yesterday
And at first it tore my heart in two
But, slowly, gradually
I let the sound of his voice
Sink into me
The tenderness of his words
Becoming one with me
"I love you" he said
His words echoing through my heart and mind
"I love you too" I whispered back
"I miss you" his voice melting into me
"I miss you too" I whispered back
And somehow
I feel him with me
Through his voice
Through his words
We are one
We are whole
My heart aches
My heart heals

Never Alone

Sometimes
It feels like we are alone
But we are not alone
The energy between us
Always there
Sometimes palpable
Sometimes just a picture in the mind
And as I lay on the ground outside
I see I am not alone
The hummingbird visits the feeder
The cat curls up by my feet
The clouds float by—the red roses bloom
I hear I am not alone
The gurgling of the fountain
The songs of the birds
The chirping of the crickets
I feel I am not alone
The energy around me and in me
Alive with words spoken and heard and read
Alive with a tender glance
A warm embrace
Sometimes it feels like we are alone
But in this world
We are never alone

A Protective Shield

There is still something about my life
That does not feel real
I go through the motions
Day in and day out
I know my son is gone
But there is something not real
Maybe I am not ready for the whole truth
And so, there is a protective shield around me
Softening the reality
Letting me breathe
Giving me time
To be in the world in this new way
Without breaking
Without coming undone
And my heart fills with gratitude
For the gentleness of the Universe
For the way life protects itself
Nurtures itself
Keeps itself safe

Where Is Hope

They say hope is part of the human experience
But where is that hope
When someone takes their own life?
When they make a mistake
That takes away everything?
And you know it was a temporary feeling
The one that drove their actions
That took them to such darkness
A darkness where there was no light
If only they had turned around
Been saved from the darkness
They would be living in the light
Glad to be alive

In the Darkness

I told my friend
That there are times
I want to keep my eyes closed
Want to stay in the darkness
Stay where it feels safe
And she said
"I think you see a lot in the darkness"
And I knew that was true
All the memories
Behind closed eyes
But there is more than my memories in the darkness
It is, for me, a place of rest
And it is a place we all need
A place of rest in the middle of things
In the middle of the chaos and the pain
It is a darkness different from "the dark night of the soul"
For there is light in this darkness
And just as after the darkness of winter
There is spring
There is growth
There is new life

To Heal

It is said
That when we heal ourselves
We heal others
For we are all connected
The life force coursing through our bodies
Through the air, the water, the earth
And when we open to our pain
Breathe through it
Witness it
Let it flow
Then there is healing
Healing for one
Healing for all

To Stay with Life

I think what I know now
Is that each day
Each moment is a choice
That becomes the path, that is the journey
One thing leads to another
And though there may be forks in the path
New directions to take
The journey is made
With each step
With each decision
With each beat of the heart
And the journey takes you where it will
But we can turn around anytime
We don't have to keep going toward some unknown destiny
We don't have to give up our life to illusion
We can keep it real
We can keep it safe
We can stay with love
Be love
We can stay with life
Be life
Be

Peace Is

I read something today
"Peace is a daily commitment"
And the truth of that
Resonated deep within my being
"Peace is a daily commitment"
A choice we make
A promise to ourselves
And to others
To the earth and to the heavens above
It comes from love
And returns to love
Peace is
Peace is a daily commitment

Holy Ground

I did it again last night
Found myself on the ground
Crying like a wounded animal
And as the tears flowed
And the moans escaped my lips
I realized
This is Holy Ground
It was my hurting self
Talking to God, to the Universe
Crying out to them
Letting them know
I needed help
I needed comfort
Letting them know
I wanted something I knew I could not have
Wanted my son back
Wanted him whole
Letting them know
I could not accept this
Could not let him go
Asking them
To hold me in this holy place
To let me cry
To let me moan
Until, once more
I could stand on Holy Ground
And say thank you
Thank you for this sacred place
This place of letting go

Watch Over You

My son ordered a watch
Four days before he died
Four days
And I wonder if he knew
How precious time is
How symbolic a watch would come to be
How, now
It seems he is watching over us
Watching and perhaps waiting
As I am
To see him again
But for now
I trust
He is watching over us
Maybe walking beside us
Keeping precious time with us

Stay

There are times
I lose my balance
My foundation so fragile
That it rocks back and forth
And it is hard to focus
Hard to stay in the present moment
Feeling as if a fog has drifted in around me
So that I cannot see clearly
Cannot see what lies beyond the fog
And I become frightened
But then I will remember
Or someone, something will remind me
I am where I belong
All I need to do is stay
Stay in the moment

Again

It's been nearly two years
Since you left
And every so often
The thought slips in
That I will not see you again
And the pain of that
Cracks my heart open again
Sends me to my knees
For I cannot bear the thought
That I will not see you again

Figuring It Out

I have come to realize
That life is about the questions we ask
And as long as I ask "why"
There is no release, no rest
But when I started asking "how"
How do I live my life
With all of this a part of it
How do I live my life
With joy
And not burdened by guilt
The answer came
You live it as you live it
You figure it out as you live into it
How you live your life
Is always where you are
And where you are
Is figuring it out

There Are Places

Someone told me today
"I see you are coming back
I can see it in your eyes"
And I am learning
That as I live into my losses
I am finding places to take care of the sadness
Places that are safe to keep the tenderness and the sorrow
So that
There are places too
Where I can learn to live again
Places where I can take my life back
Can feel the warmth and light again
Can feel peace within
A peace that "passes all understanding"

Where Is God?

There are still times
When I find myself on the floor
A broken mess
And in those times
I sometimes ask
Where is God, Love, Grace in all of this?
And the answer always comes back
She is here
Love is right here
On the floor
And when you get up
She is there
Guiding your footsteps
So that once more
You are on the path
The path that is yours
The path that takes you home
And you are always home
Even though you may wander off the path
You may find yourself on the floor
You are never lost
For home is where you are
Belonging is where you are

Hold Me

I try to be strong
I want to be strong
And maybe I am
But deep inside
My heart aches
And I want nothing more
Than to lie down
And be held
Held by strong hands
Strong hands that are tender
That will rock with me
Hold me in the silence
Until the silence opens
And I surrender
To its grace
Surrender
To its touch
Surrender once more
To truth
To hope
To peace

A New Story

Today
I sat at the foot of the cross
My hands trembling
My heart breaking
Asking God
Why my son? Why your son?
Why this darkness?
And I listened
To words of struggle
To words of hope
To words of gratitude
Wondering if I could start a new story
One that begins here
At the foot of the cross
Where everything ends
Where everything begins
At the foot of the cross
Could I stay here
Until you take my hand
And I take yours
And I walk with you
Someday
Into new life
Into light
Into peace
Into a new story

On Being Lost

I had a dream last night
I was lost
And in the dark
I kept trying to find where to go
I couldn't get a destination into my GPS
There was no such option
And I thought as I awoke
Of course
There would be no destination
Because I don't know where I'm going
I don't know where I am
So how can I be found?
How can I set my course?
But then again
They say "life is a journey
And the road is home"
So maybe
For now
I don't need to know where I am
I don't need to know where I'm going

A Quiet Place

When I swim
When I go underwater
It is so quiet there . . .
So quiet . . .
And I think
There is a place
Inside of me
Inside of each of us
Deep inside
Away from the noise, the busyness, the pain
A place that is quiet
So quiet
And if we go there
There is rest and healing
There is calm
There is peace

Angels Hovering Around

When you lose someone
There is a fog that envelops you
A fog that protects you
Hovers around you
So that
There is this tenderness around you
A gentleness
That softens the light
That muffles the sounds
And I think that maybe
Just maybe
The fog that hovers around you
Maybe
It is angels hovering around
Keeping you safe
Safe from the deepest pain of knowing
For as long as you need them
For as long as it takes
To heal enough
So that the wound of loss
Can be tended
Can be transformed
So that you can accept your life as it is
And live
Live into what comes next

Broken Enough

I want to think I am strong enough
To stay standing
When all around me is falling apart
To always begin again
No matter what has ended
To be brave enough
To keep putting one foot in front of the other
To be humble enough to be and let be
But now I realize
I am perhaps broken enough
To stay standing when I need to
To change and grow and begin again when I need to
I am broken enough
To ask for help
To know I can't do this on my own
I am broken enough
To open my mind, my heart, and my soul
To open my hands
To give love unconditionally
I am broken enough
To give
And to receive
To be grateful
For all of it

Keep Turning Pages on the Calendar

Tomorrow it will be two years since you left us
I try to think of ways to make time stop
So that you will still be here
I go back in my mind still
And make different choices
So that I could be there
Stopped it from happening somehow
I keep the calendar on July
So that
Maybe if August doesn't come
Tomorrow will not come
And you will still be here
But I know this doesn't make sense
But then nothing makes sense
Will never make sense again
And I know this is crazy talk
But that's how much I miss you
To the moon and back
To the other side of crazy and back
And for you
I will stay
And I will make sense of something
I will turn the calendar to August
Send you on your way
Keep loving you
Keep missing you
Keep living life
And somehow
Keep you close
And keep turning pages on the calendar

Love Will Find a Way

Sometimes
I still don't know how to carry on
Even though it's been two years since the impossible
    happened
Sometimes
I still find myself on the ground
Wondering how could this be
Wondering how to live my life now
And even on the darkest days
And the longest nights
I think, I believe
I have this fearless faith
That somehow
Love will make sense of this
Love will find a way
To make this right
To fill this darkness with light
Somehow
Love will find a way

Please, Please, Please

There will always be questions
When someone takes their own life
Questions that have no answers
Why? Oh my God why?
How could you?
How could you stop that beautiful heart?
How could you silence such a wonderful being?
I don't know
It cannot be understood
He had such a big heart
He lived life out loud
But I've come to believe
That my son, my beautiful son did not know what he was
     doing
He had been drinking that night
Drinking, he always told me, the way college kids do
But this time
He drank to a tipping point
When the voices in his head
The ones we all have
Turned into one voice
The stupid drunken voice
That tells lies
That tells you to do something
The other voices would never let you do
And so
If you read these words
And find yourself hearing that voice—that voice that lies
The one that tells you, you are alone
The one that tells you, you let people down

That you're broken
That you don't have what it takes
Please, please, please
Listen for the still small voice
The one that tells you
I am
I am reaching out for you
I am holding onto you
I am not letting you go
Please, please, please
Listen to that voice
Find a place to rest
Close your eyes
And wait
Please, please, please
Wait
Until the truth
Finds you
Holds you
Keeps you safe
And brings you home
Where you belong
Please, please, please

Beauty in the Heartbreak

There will always be
Beauty in the heartbreak
If we can open our hearts to see it
There will be a song
A flower
A poem
There will be someone at the door with a pan of brownies
There will be someone to hold you
To wait with you
To listen with you
To pray with you
There will always be
Beauty in the heartbreak
A hand to hold
A shoulder to lie on, to cry on
Eyes and hearts to witness the story
Arms to embrace you
Feet to walk beside you
Love to surround you
There will always be
Beauty in the heartbreak

Choose Life Again

There comes a time
In the journey of loss
When you have to choose
You have to choose life again
You still have times of deep grief
Usually at three o'clock in the morning
Or perhaps
At the cemetery
Or when the walls come crumbling down
But the rest of the time
You have to choose life
Choose things to do
That give you a sense of being alive
Choose people to be with
Who give you a sense of being alive
Because then
Maybe
You'll stop just going through the motions
And you'll live the life you've been given with its loss
        and its heartbreak
But you'll live it
With a sense of being alive

32141450R00162

Made in the USA
San Bernardino, CA
29 March 2016

A New Story

Today
I sat at the foot of the cross
My hands trembling
My heart breaking
Asking God
Why my son? Why your son?
Why this darkness?
And I listened
To words of struggle
To words of hope
To words of gratitude
Wondering if I could start a new story
One that begins here
At the foot of the cross
Where everything ends
Where everything begins
At the foot of the cross
Could I stay here
Until you take my hand
And I take yours
And I walk with you
Someday
Into new life
Into light
Into peace
Into a new story